WAR CRIMES AND
THE AMERICAN CONSCIENCE

WAR CRIMES AND THE AMERICAN CONSCIENCE

EDITED BY

ERWIN KNOLL

AND

JUDITH NIES McFADDEN

HOLT, RINEHART AND WINSTON
NEW YORK   CHICAGO   SAN FRANCISCO

Published simultaneously in Canada by Holt, Rinehart
and Winston of Canada, Limited.

Library of Congress Catalog Card Number: 76-122254

FIRST EDITION

SBN (Hardbound): 03-085329-X
SBN (Paperback): 03-085328-l

Designer: Christine Aulicino

Printed in the United States of America

CONTENTS

PREFACE   vii

INTRODUCTION:
Individual Responsibility and Collective Guilt   xi
*by Representatives George E. Brown, Jr., Philip
Burton, John Conyers, Jr., Robert C. Eckhardt, Don
Edwards, Donald M. Fraser, Robert W. Kasten-
meier, Abner J. Mikva, Benjamin S. Rosenthal, and
William F. Ryan*

I. LAW, MORALITY AND WAR:
The Ideals of Nuremberg   1

II. TECHNOLOGY AND AMERICAN POWER:
The Changing Nature of War   47

III. AMERICANS IN VIETNAM:
The Lessons of My Lai   104

IV. INDIVIDUAL CONSCIENCE:
The Moral Challenge   149

APPENDIXES
1. Principles of Nuremberg   182
2. Excerpts from Department of the Army Field
Manual, *The Law of Land Warfare*   184
3. Treaties to Which the United States Is a Party   193
4. Excerpts from the Supreme Court Opinion in *The
Matter of Yamashita*   194
5. Majority Judgment of the Tokyo War Crimes
Tribunal   195

NOTES ON THE CONTRIBUTORS   197

PREFACE

It would have been inconceivable only a few years ago that a serious and searching discussion of war crimes—including American war crimes—could be conducted under Congressional auspices at the Capitol of the United States. Traditionally, each nation denounces the "war crimes" of its enemies, while justifying its own conduct in time of war, no matter how flagrantly that conduct may violate established standards of law and morality. But the disastrous continuation of the war in Southeast Asia and the disclosure of the massacre at My Lai have raised many Americans to a new level of consciousness—and conscience—about the policies pursued by their Government and the actions that flow from those policies.

One manifestation of this new, overdue concern was the Congressional Conference on War and National Responsibility, convened in Washington early in 1970. The Congressional sponsors were Representatives George E. Brown, Jr., and Phillip Burton of California, John Conyers, Jr., of Michigan, Robert C. Eckhardt of Texas, Don Edwards of California, Donald M. Fraser of Minnesota, Robert W. Kastenmeier of Wisconsin, Abner J. Mikva of Illinois, and Benjamin S. Rosenthal and William F. Ryan of New York. At their invitation, a group of leading American scholars, jurists, and public figures assembled at the Capitol for two days of intensive deliberation. Some came as recognized authorities on the legal and moral aspects of modern warfare. Others reported on their own experiences and observations in Vietnam. Also participating in this remarkable colloquy were members of the Congressional sponsoring group, as well as Senator George

McGovern of South Dakota and Representatives Jonathan
B. Bingham and Richard D. McCarthy of New York,
Henry S. Reuss of Wisconsin, Louis Stokes of Ohio, and
Jerome R. Waldie of California.

This book consists of an edited transcript of the Conference proceedings and supplementary material contributed by the participants. In addition, Professor
George Wald, Dr. Jerome Frank, and Professor Charles C.
Moskos, Jr., who were unable to attend the Conference,
submitted prepared statements for inclusion in this
volume. Some basic documents of international and national war crimes law appear in the Appendix. The Congressional sponsors were eager to have the official
viewpoint of the armed services represented at the Conference, and extended invitations to the Judge Advocates
General of the Army, Navy, and Air Force. Regrettably,
these invitations were declined. Replying in behalf of all
three Judge Advocates General, Rear Admiral Joseph B.
McDevitt cited "the sensitive positions we fill in the administration of military justice and [the fact] that many
issues which undoubtedly will be discussed at the Conference are presently in litigation."

The Conference was the third in a series held under the
aegis of essentially the same group of Congressmen. The
first, in January, 1966, arrived at an extraordinarily pro-
phetic assessment of the Vietnam war and a strong appeal
for de-escalation which was, tragically, ignored at the
time. The second, a symposium on the Military Budget
and National Priorities, was held in the spring of 1969,
and played a significant part in the widening national
debate on the proper allocation of America's resources; it
was published in book form as *American Militarism: 1970*
by the Viking Press. Like these earlier efforts, the 1970
Conference dealt with questions of the most urgent public
interest and merits the broadest attention and discussion.

The editors gratefully acknowledge the cooperation of

the Conference participants and the valuable counsel of Marcus Raskin.

ERWIN KNOLL
JUDITH NIES MCFADDEN

Washington, D.C.
May 1970

INTRODUCTION:

Individual Responsibility and Collective Guilt

What individual responsibility does the soldier, the military commander, the government bureaucrat, the elected political leader, and the ordinary citizen bear for illegal and immoral policies and actions undertaken by his nation? To what extent are governments and individuals bound by domestic or international law in time of war? What is the significance of the Nuremberg and Asian war crimes trials to the United States today? What moral and legal challenges facing Americans were illuminated by the massacre at My Lai?

As Members of Congress, we brought together a distinguished panel in Washington early in 1970 to shed the light of their collective knowledge on these and other questions involved in a central issue of our times—modern warfare as exemplified by Vietnam and other "small wars" that have afflicted our planet since 1945.

The focus of their discourse was Vietnam, but the questions they raise apply as well to Algeria, to Biafra, to Hungary, to Tibet, to any one of the thirty-seven nations that have been involved in alleged war crimes and atrocities since World War II.

We thought we had disposed of the question of individual responsibility and collective guilt in the Nuremberg trials. The My Lai massacre serves as a dramatic reminder of how naïve and self-righteous was that assumption. Our panel re-examined the question in the light of Vietnam, and its implications both for the future of the United States and the survival of the human race.

In the pages that follow, for example, panelist Richard Falk points out that acts committed in the name of the American people in Vietnam "are not only violations of the laws of war, but . . . constitute what the United States itself regarded as acts of barbarism when they were performed by other governments."

In "Operation Cedar Falls," named after the hometown of a Medal of Honor winner, 30,000 American troops were assigned the task of destroying all of the villages in a forty-square-mile area named (by us) the "Iron Triangle." The villages in that area were invaded, the inhabitants evacuated, the houses and fields burned. The men were considered (by us) to be Vietcong and the women and children "hostile civilians" to be "relocated" to nonexistent "settlement camps."

Under the guidance and direction of American "advisers," the South Vietnamese have conducted "Operation Phoenix," a program officially described as "an attack on the Vietcong infrastructure" but widely acknowledged to be a scheme of systematic assassination.

We have been protected by such euphemistic code names as "free-fire zone," "search and destroy," and "hostile civilians" from knowing that My Lai was unique only in the way it came to public attention and in the number of people involved.

We beguile ourselves when we think we have solved the problem of responsibility by bringing legal action against a few individuals. "This is," points out panelist Hans Morgenthau, "psychologically convenient, because once a man has been tried and convicted, we can all say we have recognized the evil done by this man—not by us—in spite of all the instructions to the contrary. Then we can carry on as before, with our consciences relieved. . . . It is the war itself, the kind of war we are waging, and the purposes for which we are waging it, which is at fault. And, insofar as the nature of the war is at fault, we are all at fault."

The changing nature of war raises the questions of when, and how, and under what conditions we may legitimately become involved. What are brush-fire wars? What are limited wars? What are wars of national liberation? By what authority can these wars be carried out under international law, and when, if ever, may we justifiably intervene?

The Vietnam war has spread to all of Indo-China, and we teeter on the brink of other Vietnams. The world is increasingly in ferment. Given our disposition to see in each crisis a threat to our security, given our propensity to seek military solutions, we will be hard-pressed to avoid other Vietnams. Other My Lais are likely, and they will not necessarily be limited to foreign soil. If violations of the laws of war are tacitly accepted by our Government, the total integrity of society is called into question. To destroy the "enemy" you must first dehumanize him, make him less than human. And that dehumanization in Vietnam—with its implications of racism—is producing visible consequences in our own society, feeding the breakdown of respect for law and the increasing reliance on violence to deal with domestic problems.

The technology of modern war predisposes us toward dehumanization. It is no longer considered a war crime or atrocity to kill a thousand civilians with bombs or napalm, to starve them through the use of defoliants, to flush them from their lairs with gas.

At what point does the game become not worth the candle? At what point, in short, do we lose our souls in pursuit of a military objective?

To those who would say the destruction of civilian

populations is necessary to protect the lives of our own men in such actions as Vietnam, our reply is: If that is the case, we should never have gone there in the first place. And we must, at all cost, avoid other Vietnams.

We sponsored this discussion in the belief that we can rise above the mistakes of the past. Our best hope of doing so lies with an informed public prepared to assert its will on those who make policy. With that hope in mind, we offer the deliberations that follow.

> Representatives
> George E. Brown, Jr.
> Phillip Burton
> John Conyers, Jr.
> Robert C. Eckhardt
> Don Edwards
> Donald M. Fraser
> Robert W. Kastenmeier
> Abner J. Mikva
> Benjamin S. Rosenthal
> William F. Ryan

WAR CRIMES AND
THE AMERICAN CONSCIENCE

I

LAW, MORALITY, AND WAR:

The Ideals of Nuremberg

afirm or deny!

"If certain acts in violation of treaties are crimes, they are crimes whether the United States does them or whether Germany does them, and we are not prepared to lay down a rule of criminal conduct against others which we would be unwilling to have invoked against us."

—**JUSTICE ROBERT JACKSON**
Chief United States Prosecutor at Nuremberg

REPRESENTATIVE DON EDWARDS: At the end of World War II, the nations that had been allied in combat against Nazi Germany and Imperial Japan established the precedent in the Nuremberg and Tokyo trials that men must accept responsibility for their conduct during war. At that time, Senator Robert A. Taft, in a controversial speech at Kenyon College, expressed his doubts about the value of the precedent:

> Peace in the world can only come if a law is agreed to relating to international relations, if there is a tribunal which can interpret that law and decide disputes between nations, and if the nations are willing to submit their dis-

putes to impartial decisions regardless of the outcome. There can be no peace until the public opinion of the world accepts as a matter of course the decisions of an international tribunal. . . . I question whether the hanging of those, who, however despicable, were the leaders of the German people will ever discourage the making of aggressive wars, for no one makes aggressive war unless he expects to win.

The historic record since 1945 demonstrates Senator Taft's wisdom. An incomplete study of alleged war crimes and atrocities committed since the end of World War II details 144 incidents involving thirty-seven nations or groups. Even a casual glance at the nature of armed conflict since 1945 shows technological and tactical changes that have made warfare more horrible. Examples are everywhere—in Vietnam, which has been continuously at war since 1945; in the Algerian-French conflict; in Biafra; in the Chinese invasion of Tibet; in the Soviet Union's actions in Hungary and Czechoslovakia. The list is almost endless.

Certainly there have been no internationally enforceable standards for the conduct of war since 1945. But at Nuremberg and Tokyo, some of the nations of the world, including the United States, attempted to forge such standards. They may, indeed, have forged a two-edged sword, violating the biblical injunction, "Judge not, lest ye be judged."

One of the questions we must face is whether there is such a thing as a war crime or whether the only crime of war is that of losing. History appears to affirm the latter position, but I, for one, must insist on the former. I believe that we as a people, as a nation, must set standards for our conduct, even if in doing so we stand alone in the world. One man, one nation, must take the first step if mankind is to live up to its promise as a humane and reasoning species.

Three developments since 1945 have made it extremely difficult to define rules for the conduct of armed conflicts:

1. The formal declaration of war has become a rarity. The United States has fought in Korea, in Vietnam, and elsewhere on this globe without declaring war. Other nations, large and small, our allies and our opponents, have followed the same course. As a result, it is difficult to establish responsibility for any specific conflict. I remind you of the changing parties to the conflict in Vietnam, a conflict now in its twenty-fifth year. Furthermore, we are faced with conflicts called "wars of national liberation" which may or may not be limited to nationals of the country involved. Outside intervention in what are essentially civil wars has widened, prolonged, and intensified conflicts that might have been settled rather quickly by the parties directly involved. Clearly, we must re-examine our definitions of war and our reasons for participating in it.

2. The tactics of terror have become an essential tactic of war. We no longer have uniformed armies facing each other across identifiable lines. Instead, masses of civilians —including women and children—are used as the pawns of war. In Algeria, in the Arab-Israeli conflicts, in Vietnam, terror has been used by rebels, and those forces attempting to suppress insurrection have often resorted to counter-terror. In an unstructured war, waged to gain control of civilian populations, the old rules of war dating back to the Middle Ages have been discarded.

3. During the Spanish Civil War and in the early days of World War II, Nazi Germany was charged with war crimes because of its aerial bombardment of civilian populations. Yet such bombardment is common today, dating back to the Allied use of such mass bombing tactics against Germany and Japan. It is no longer considered a war crime or atrocity to kill a thousand civilians with a

bomb or napalm, although it is still considered a crime or atrocity to kill one civilian with a pistol. We have developed sophisticated new weapons—chemicals to defoliate vegetation, gases to flush out an enemy, drugs to break down the resistance of prisoners.

As this dark record has unfolded, nations engaged in combat have been content to publicize their enemies' atrocities while concealing or condoning their own. The game might well be called "Your War Crime Is Bigger Than Mine."

It is not our purpose to play that game of accusing others or even ourselves. Our purpose is to examine international, national, and individual responsibility for armed conflict and its conduct. Even so, we may be undertaking an unpopular task: The polls show the American people resent the charges brought against United States troops for conduct in Vietnam—resent not only the charges, but those who report those charges. It is not our task to investigate those charges or to draw conclusions about specific incidents or individuals. But we do work under the shadow of the massacre at My Lai, and we do work in the context of American responsibility for the conduct of this nation's armed forces. And our concern is not only with our conduct, but with our conscience.

RICHARD FALK: The basic issue that arises when we consider the application of the laws of war to the situation in Vietnam is the recognition that our military capabilities are not suited to the political and military mission that they have been assigned. Furthermore, the efforts to fulfill that mission almost inevitably involve the systematic and massive reliance on battlefield tactics that not only are violations of the laws of war, but constitute what the United States itself regarded as acts of barbarism when they were performed by other governments. Therefore, the broader significance of our inquiry is the contradiction between large-scale counterinsurgency warfare and a minimal and decent respect for the opinions of mankind and the laws of war.

The dramatic disclosure of the My Lai massacre in November, 1969, gave a new focus to the war crimes issue as it applies to the Vietnam war. The evidence advanced in support of the commission of a massive atrocity by American troops participating in the attack against My Lai No. 4 hamlet of Song My village on March 16, 1968, was so vivid and persuasive that it captured the attention of the public. But long before these disclosures there was abundant evidence that the United States was committing war crimes in Vietnam on a widespread and continuing basis. Much of this evidence was gathered together in a book called *In the Name of America*, sponsored by some of the most prominent religious leaders in the United States and published in 1968 under the auspices of the Clergy and Laymen Concerned About Vietnam—months before the My Lai massacre took place. There have been many authenticated accounts of specific atrocities committed by the armed forces of the United States in such South Vietnamese villages as Lang Vei, Dien Quang, Tinh Son, An Phuoc in the Binh Son district, and in Quang Ngai province.

More serious than the widespread occurrence of these atrocities, however, is the official reliance by the United States Government on a set of battlefield policies that openly deny the significance of any distinction between civilians and combatants, between military and nonmilitary targets. The most spectacular of these practices are the B-52 pattern raids against undefended villages and populated areas, "free-fire zones," "harassment and interdiction fire," "Operation Phoenix," "search-and-destroy" missions, massive crop destruction and defoliation, and forcible transfer of the civilian population in Vietnam from one place to another against their will.

Viewed in this light, the events at My Lai were not unusual, and it is a grave distortion of the way in which the war in Vietnam is being conducted to repudiate the acts of individual soldiers at My Lai and yet to continue bombing villages every day from thirty thousand feet, where the people on the ground can neither see nor hear the planes and only know they are being attacked when the explosions take place on the ground.

In fact, the wrongdoers at My Lai, whether or not they were carrying out specific command decisions, were indeed fulfilling the basic and persistent United States war policies in South Vietnam. My first principal point, then, is that the circle of criminal responsibility drawn around participants in the massacre at My Lai is far too narrow to be significant. In fact, it may be deceptive, since it allows our political and military leaders to repudiate the kind of barbarism for which their own leadership is responsible on a day-to-day basis.

There is no way to support the continuation of large-scale American participation in the Vietnam war without knowingly committing war crimes. The evidence is so abundant and so unambiguous that war crimes *are* being committed in Vietnam by the United States Government that there is no longer any excuse for silence or acquiescence on the part of American citizens. These war crimes are being committed in our name and in our behalf, and it is our legal right and duty to stop them by all possible means.

Franklin Delano Roosevelt, toward the end of World War II, issued the following appeal to the German people: "Hitler is committing these crimes against humanity in the name of the German people. I ask every German and every man everywhere under Nazi domination to show the world that he does not share these insane criminal

desires.... I ask him also to keep watch, and to record the evidence that will one day be used to convict the guilty."
A similar appeal to the American people by responsible leaders is long overdue.

More than any other country, the United States struggled at Nuremberg and afterwards to bring about a new era of international law. Statesmen and leaders were to be held responsible for initiating an illegal war or conducting a war in an illegal manner. The United States persuaded the Soviet Union that the prosecution of German and Japanese war leaders should be based on *general principles* of international law, not on a special set of rules framed to reach just these particular individuals. Justice Robert Jackson, Chief United States Prosecutor at Nuremberg, stated the issue clearly: "If certain acts in violation of treaties are crimes, they are crimes whether the United States does them or whether Germany does them, and we are not prepared to lay down a rule of criminal conduct against others which we would be unwilling to have invoked against us."

The experience of Nuremberg was given the unanimous endorsement of the United Nations at its first General Assembly meeting in a resolution that called upon the International Law Commission of the United Nations to formulate the principles of international law embodied in the Nuremberg Judgment. After several years of inquiry and discussion, the International Law Commission formulated seven principles governing individual criminal responsibility that still constitute the most authoritative summary of the Nuremberg experience. The United States Army Field Manual issued in 1956 over the signature of General Maxwell Taylor makes explicit the overriding obligation of soldiers to respect the laws of war as embodied in a series of international treaties, ratified by the United States and entitled by our Constitution to the status of the supreme law of the land.

It seems clear, then, that both combat officers who order or commit war crimes and leaders who plan and approve illegal war policies are criminally responsible for their acts if the positions that we helped to evolve at Nuremberg are to be taken seriously. The United States Supreme Court, in *The Matter of Yamashita*, made it very clear that a commanding officer—in this case a Japanese general in command of the Philippines theater—was criminally responsible for abuses of civilians committed by soldiers under his command even if he did not order these acts and had no specific knowledge of their character or occurrence. General Yamashita's conviction was upheld by the Supreme Court because he was expected to control the troops under his command. By American orders, General Yamashita was put to death for this passive dereliction of duty.

The purpose of emphasizing the commission of war crimes by the United States in Vietnam is to call for the repudiation of these policies in decisive and effective terms. The presentation of evidence of war crimes does not have a punitive objective; it is not intended to punish those who have committed these crimes nearly so much as it is to educate the public about the character of this activity and its departure from moral and legal standards that we claim to respect and uphold. Without the exposure of these Vietnam policies as criminal, there is every likelihood of their repetition in subsequent conflicts.

TELFORD TAYLOR: Those to whom the Vietnam war in its entirety is an abomination may find any consideration of the laws of war, and what may or may not be done legitimately in military operations, to be questions of small account. But a majority of Americans do not regard our involvement in Vietnam as criminal, whatever they may now think about the desirability of withdrawal. And it is the American public as a whole, not just the opponents of the war, who must confront the difficult issues raised by the conduct of American operations in Vietnam. These issues transcend arguments about the wisdom or legality of our presence in Vietnam. They center on the ways and means by which that presence is now being exerted and on the methods by which our Government is carrying out its policies. The question which gives rise to our concern is whether those methods are defensible in law, in morality, in policy, or in any terms whatever.

The laws of war are written in very general terms, and the means for their enforcement leave much to be desired. They must be based primarily on the concept of what is reasonably necessary for operations. Rules of war that interfere significantly with military success do not remain enforceable. We must recognize therefore that the enforcement of the laws of war—enforcement that would commend itself to our sense of justice—must correspond to the realities.

The laws of war are also highly circumstantial in their enforcement. As Congressman Edwards has recalled, Nazi Germany was denounced in the press during World War II for its aerial bombardment of civilian populations. However, no such charges were brought at Nuremberg, and the reason was obvious enough: By the time the war crimes trials took place, the practices on both sides had altered to the point where any effort to enforce such a rule, even though founded in the Hague Conventions, would have seemed ridiculous.

To cite another example, it is a Hague rule that one is not supposed to deny quarter: One is supposed to take prisoners. Anyone who has been much involved in military operations knows that circumstances arise when that is not done because it becomes dangerous, difficult, or even impossible to do what the rules require.

Because of these admitted and inevitable problems

posed by the rules of war, it has been argued, with some
show of reason, that any effort to enforce limitations on
military combat is doomed to failure—that the rules themselves are futile, hypocritical, or worse. This argument has
been made for decades, even for centuries, but it does not
seem to me that it is a valid one.

There are at least two basic reasons why some effort
must be made to preserve and enforce the rules of war.
The first reason is pragmatic: The fact is that with all of
their shortcomings they work in terms of saving human
life. Millions of people are alive today because the rules
with respect to prisoners of war were followed in World
War II. There is not the slightest question that life is saved
by even a partial observance of the rules.

The second reason is, I think, more basic: It has to do
with the effect of war on the people who engage in it. It
is one thing to say to a man who puts on a uniform and
goes into combat that he is permitted to kill for the purpose of achieving military success. It is quite another thing
to say he is entitled to kill anybody at any time in any way
he pleases. If men are permitted and indeed encouraged
to behave that way, there is not the slightest assurance
they will not continue to behave that way when they
return from the war.

In other words, some effort to maintain a degree of
civilization, even in the conduct of war, is essential if we
are to preserve the distinction between peace and war.

The application of these generalities to the war in Vietnam has been especially difficult for reasons with which
we are all familiar—the nature of the terrain, the preva-
lence of guerrilla warfare, the fact that women and children engage in combat, the problem of distinguishing
friend from foe.

But these very difficulties underline the force of what
should be the first and imperative principle of our conduct
in Vietnam—to preserve, by all possible means, the well-

being of the country we claim to be protecting. This is required by the laws and principles to which we committed ourselves at Nuremberg and, indeed, many years before Nuremberg. It is required by the morality which our country espouses and the standards of common humanity to which all nations may rightly be held accountable. It is required by ordinary common sense, for we are in Vietnam in the name of international security, and we stultify and discredit our announced aims by heedless slaughter and destruction.

One feature of the rules of war which struck me most forcibly at Nuremberg was that the violations charged to Nazi Germany did not, on the whole, pay dividends in terms of victory or defeat. They were usually counterproductive.

One of the trials at Nuremberg was concerned with a situation not totally unlike Vietnam—the occupation of the Balkan countries by German troops from 1941 to 1945. As in Vietnam, the population was partly friendly, partly hostile, partly neutral, and the occupying forces were confronted with difficult problems of what they, too, called "pacification."

In 1941, shortly after the Germans went in, a German lieutenant colonel in Belgrade reported to his commanding officer that the widespread reprisals being carried out were stirring up the population and were being welcomed by the Communists against whom the Germans were contending.

A few months later, an official of the German ministry of the Interior wrote this report on the reprisals and killing of hostages:

> The consequences of the practices being carried out by our troops will be that a large number of innocent people will be slaughtered and the Communists in the woods will increase in numbers, because many farmers, even entire vil-

lages, even though up to now they had no connection with the Communists, will flee into the woods out of fear and will be received there by the Communists. This will develop on a large scale and will have incalculable and terrible consequences for the entire population.

Two years later the German plenipotentiary in the Balkans protested to the German Air Force against the bombing of villages from which there had been sniping and other hostile activities, contending that on the whole these bombings forced additional people to join the insurrectionists and, as he put it, "shake the confidence in German soldiers on the part of those parts of the population which are of good will."

I will cite one more example, involving an episode in the Greek town of Klissura. In April, 1944, two German soldiers were killed a few miles from that village. The German troops in the neighborhood thereupon burned the village and killed all of the inhabitants, to the number of 223, including 50 who were under ten years old and 128 women and old men.

The German minister in the Balkans protested to the German commanding general in these terms:

It is sheer insanity to shoot babies, children, women, and old people because heavily armed Reds had been boarded in their houses for one night and had shot the German soldiers in the neighborhood. The political consequences of such deeds may be very serious. It is obviously easier to kill harmless children and old men and women than to hunt down an armed band. I demand a thorough investigation.

The investigation was made and the military reply strikes a familiar note; it was that there had been no retaliatory reprisal—that the village had been taken by storm and the inhabitants killed by artillery fire.

Evidence is accumulating in Vietnam that our leaders, like the Germans in World War II, are losing sight of elementary truths. The evidence suggests the strong possibility that the lives of the inhabitants of Vietnam are held as of little value and are sacrificed carelessly, wantonly, and even sportively, and that the country is being physically ravaged far beyond the range of reasonable military necessity. There is serious cause for concern that our leaders have become so immersed in the business of war that they are blind to the ends for which we went to Vietnam in the first place, and that our troops will come to be feared and hated perhaps more than the forces against whom they are supposed to be protecting the people.

These issues cannot be resolved by court-martial proceedings involving a few officers and men. They deeply involve the command structure, both political and military, of the entire Vietnamese undertaking. There is little reason to think that self-scrutiny by the military agencies, whether through the Inspector-General or other branches, is an effective check.

It is Congress that appropriates the money for and determines the organization of the military establishment. The President's responsibilities as Commander-in-Chief must, of course, be respected, but Congress, too, has its responsibilities, as well as powers and prerogatives for their discharge. During World War II, a continuing scrutiny of the Executive's conduct of operations was undertaken by the committee headed by the then Senator Harry S. Truman. Confronted as the Congress now is by issues as momentous as those we are considering, the Congress, or either of its Houses, might wisely decide to establish a committee of investigation, armed with the necessary powers for their full exploration.

HANS MORGENTHAU: There is a widespread opinion that what is happening in Vietnam is "just a war" and that "war is like that." I think this is a misunderstanding of the history of warfare. One can go back to the Middle Ages and find that this kind of systematic, indiscriminate killing, with the body count as the measure of success, has virtually no parallel in the modern history of warfare.

In other, less sophisticated times—in the sixteenth century—Machiavelli, who was not particularly sentimental about such matters, wrote a history of warfare and reported a battle in which one man was killed—and he fell off his horse.

In the eighteenth century, we have the letters of Lord Chesterfield to his son, who complained about the civilized character of warfare. He said there were no longer any sieges of fortresses, no longer any mass battles, nobody was killing anybody, and even women were deprived of the benefit of rape. In other words, what we have now in Vietnam is a radical departure from the practices of warfare which were observed for a very long time.

To cite another example, in the War of 1870 between Prussia and France, when some French citizens—the so-called *franc tireurs*—took to the woods and started shooting, there was great controversy over whether to deal with them as prisoners of war or as illegal murderers. And this controversy raged not in France, but in Germany.

Finally, when World War II started, both the President and the Secretary of State of the United States were incensed at the bombardment of Warsaw by the German Air Force—though this war ended with the routine destruction of Cologne, Hamburg, Dresden, Hiroshima, and Nagasaki.

The second point I want to make is of a legal and political nature: I really don't think one can usefully argue about what we are doing in Vietnam in terms of the Hague

Conference or the international treaties concluded in the 1920s or the principles of the Nuremberg trials. It is the nature of the Vietnam war itself which makes what we are doing there inevitable. We are not fighting an army. We are not even fighting a group of partisans in the woods, as the Germans did in Yugoslavia. We are fighting an entire people. And since everyone in the countryside of Vietnam is to a lesser or greater degree our potential enemy, it is perfectly logical to kill everyone in sight.

Therefore, it is not the responsibility of a particular general or of a particular lieutenant that is at stake here, but it is the responsibility—the political and moral responsibility—of our Government, which wages a war that inevitably will lead to the mass destruction of the South Vietnamese population.

When we talk about the violation of the rules of war, we must keep in mind that the fundamental violation, from which all other specific violations follow, is the very waging of this kind of war.

ROBERT JAY LIFTON: I would like to examine a point made by Professor Taylor. It is true, of course, that the rules of war follow realities of war. But once one says that, it seems to me essential to look at the nature of the "reality." Realities are not something bequeathed to us by some outside force; they are man-made. Therefore, the reality itself could be, as in the case of the Vietnam war, absurd and evil.

In such a case the task—the ethical task—becomes not to adapt oneself to that reality, but rather to transform it. Just as the reality itself was made by man, it takes men to transform and change the reality.

A second point is that wars might have had a kind of logic and a proneness to follow rules prior to the development of high technology. Technology has a direct influence, I think, upon the capacity to make workable rules of war. The conclusion one is driven to is that all wars at a time of high technology tend to defy rules and create absurd and evil situations. They are easily conducted without any sense of rules and without any sense of hostility toward the enemy, in a state of what I would call psychic numbing or desensitization as protected and maintained by the technology.

In this sense the nature of present-day warfare, and the war in Vietnam in particular, must make all of us more radical in our examination and criticisms of these realities created by man.

TELFORD TAYLOR: I have no basic quarrel with that analysis, but I would like to carry it a bit further. There are many realities in any situation. A very important reality in World War II was that for the most part the American people regarded the waging of the war and the achievement of victory as essential and right. Therefore, there was high tolerance for a degree of violence in achieving that objective. That is a reason, I suppose, why there was not at the time more outcry against the change in aerial tactics that led to the bombardment of large population centers.

This works in reverse, as well. If one's attitude toward the war is intrinsically negative, one's level of toleration is prone to be lower.

Dr. Morgenthau takes the position, as indeed many do, that the nature of this war itself is the evil, and one cannot expect to think of Hague Conventions and other limitations because the war itself is at fault. This may well be so, but the fact of the matter is that a majority of the American people do not think so. It may be that the most important task is to persuade them to that view, but it seems to me we ought to address ourselves here not only to people who think that the entire war is a criminal abomination, but to the majority, silent or not, who do not, and try to make them aware of the consequences of the way this war is being waged. That, too, is a reality.

RICHARD BARNET: I agree that the only real basis on which the people of this country are going to turn away from war is proof that war is, in itself, self-defeating. It also seems clear to me that it is impossible to fight the kind of war we are fighting in Vietnam and Laos and many other places without the commission of war crimes. But the United States has justified its policy of worldwide counter-insurgency on the basis that intervention in such revolutionary situations is vital to its national security. So long as there is a consensus in this country that this is true, we will not be able to overcome the consensus that supports the war.

We need the broadest public discussion of that issue—of the nature of our society and the way it has defined its security requirements. I don't think it is at all too early—in fact, it may already be too late—for serious people to begin this kind of discussion, recognizing that the issues of legality that we have discussed really do revolve around the issue of what the United States is and what it is going to be.

BENJAMIN V. COHEN: We must recognize that there has been a basic difference of opinion in the past on how our Government should operate in the field of foreign affairs and in the waging of war. Many have argued that foreign affairs and the waging of war are matters too intricate and complex to be shared with the people, and that these matters must be decided by an elite with as little public debate and disclosure as possible.

This is where many of our difficulties have arisen. If we believe in democracy, we must agree that important matters of foreign affairs and war—matters for which people are asked to give their lives—should be publicly explored and discussed as long before the time for decision arrives or a crisis occurs as is possible.

At scarcely any step of the Vietnam war was the Congress or the American people informed of all the factors involved. I am convinced the American people did not realize the character of the war they were getting into or the nature or causes of our involvement. Emergencies arose, midnight decisions were made by the President with the assistance of the State and Defense Departments, and the Congress and the people were asked to suppress their doubts and not to let down their President, who was better informed than they were.

I do not share the view that Vietnam proves we need a weaker Executive and a stronger Congress; in my view, it would be a calamity if we did not have a strong President and an informed and inquiring Congress in this twentieth century. But all strong Presidents are not necessarily good, wise, or responsible Presidents. We need not a dictatorial President, but a President who has a sense of responsibility not only to the Congress but to the people and who feels that part of his job is to carry the people with him on the basis of full and timely disclosure.

The recent resolution of the Senate calling for congressional approval of the use of our armed forces in armed conflict is quite inadequate to meet the situation. The Congress did approve the Tonkin Bay Resolution authorizing the use of force in Southeast Asia. Senator J. William Fulbright himself sponsored the resolution because action was asked to meet an alleged emergency without Congress having the knowledge or opportunity to consider alternative courses of action or the time to inquire into the facts. The Congress had to support or repudiate the President in a crisis without full knowledge of the facts or circumstances. What is needed is timely consultation and disclosure before the Executive Branch becomes publicly committed to a specific course of action. As Senator Arthur Vandenberg was wont to say, the Congress and the people should be informed and consulted before the take-off and not merely on the crash-landing.

MARCUS RASKIN: At the end of World War I there was, of course, a major international debate about the outlawing of war itself. Aggressive war was viewed as a crime in and of itself. As I understand it, this turned out to be a very important part of the case against the German leaders at Nuremberg—that they had waged a war of aggression.

In the late 1920s, the Senate debated the Borah Resolution, which held that it was a crime to organize or preach war. It had strong support in the Senate at that time, although it was not passed.

These are ancient problems, and from time to time people have hoped they had enough political and public support to bring them to the fore. To some extent, that sort of energy has served as the basis of attempts to develop a new sort of domestic and international law on the subject.

The problem in the United States now, it seems to me, is not that there is a lack of law, but that there is a fear of attempting to apply it or, more particularly, a sense that it really is too late. Once everyone becomes convinced that there is a contradiction between creed and conduct, it may very well be the case that people will not choose creed. They may, instead, choose a far more expedient conclusion—that this is who we are, this is the way we fight, if you don't like it here, get out.

JAMES ARMSTRONG: Milton Mayer says flatly, "Nuremberg was a sham." That is not true. Surely the Principles of Nuremberg have exercised a restraining influence over the conduct of war and, on occasion, have encouraged dissent. But Nuremberg has been happily ignored by the C.I.A., "official" investigating teams, and the Administration-of-your-choice. Though we may appeal to sweeping investigations and trials, freedom does not find its ultimate security in legal procedures, as Chicago has so recently pointed out, or in formal precedent, as Nuremberg painfully reminds us.

TELFORD TAYLOR: I don't know whether the actions of the C.I.A. prove that Nuremberg or the C.I.A. is a "sham." I suppose they do establish what all of us know—that men often declare principles and then find themselves unable to live up to them.

Rather more complicated is the matter of Auschwitz as contrasted with Hiroshima—a matter which, incidentally, was extensively discussed at Nuremberg. Whatever the defects there, this problem was not overlooked, although it may not have been dealt with as effectively as it should have been. Some have suggested that it was Hiroshima, rather than Auschwitz, that led to the problem of atomic warfare that confronts the world today. I don't really know whether it was Hiroshima or Alamogordo that set off this problem. What the result would have been if the atom bomb had been developed but never dropped is a speculation that surpasses my wisdom. I simply do not know. I suppose the problem arose from the development of the bomb in the first place. Perhaps, in that sense, Fermi and Oppenheimer and the others who developed the bomb were the greater criminals than those who organized Auschwitz, but this is a conclusion that seems to me to rob the appellation of criminality of any meaning that we can all accept. As for the dropping of the bomb on Hiroshima, I am not clear why this was a greater crime than the bombing of Tokyo. In quantitative terms, the loss of life in Tokyo was higher than in Hiroshima.

Whatever the rights and wrongs of Hiroshima, I don't suppose anyone would suggest that once we had won the war we were going to continue dropping atomic bombs. Auschwitz, on the other hand, was one of the purposes of the Germans in waging war, and it would have continued if they had won.

There is a tendency to approach not only Nuremberg but the law in general as if it were a much more exact and perfect science than it is. Morality is what we conceive as proper conduct, and we can be held to a measure of consistency in the development of moral principles. But law is a social enterprise. It stems from statutes enacted by legislatures which are inhabited by the need to compromise. It is applied by judges, juries, defense counsel, prosecution counsel. It is an imperfect process. Doctors fail to cure the sick, clergymen fail to save souls, and lawyers often fail to do justice. It is too much to expect the legal process to be consistent or principled or perfect all the time; if it meets these tests a fair share of the time, we have done a good deal better than used to be done.

I would suggest, therefore, that we are putting Nuremberg to much too severe a test. On balance, the pressures from Nuremberg have been good rather than bad. The very fact that we can point to inconsistencies and accuse ourselves in terms of Nuremberg is good rather than bad, it seems to me.

We find Nuremberg invoked for the most extraordinary opposite positions. Secretary of State Dean Rusk never, so far as I can recall, specifically cited Nuremberg, but the general principle against aggressive war—based on the Nuremberg idea—was used to justify our intervention in Vietnam. The North Vietnamese invoke Nuremberg as a possible basis for trying American aviators. And those who are confronting the draft appeal to Nuremberg as the basis for not consenting to serve.

Maybe this shows that Nuremberg is indeed a very vague thing, but the mere fact that it is invoked for inconsistent aims does not seem to me to destroy its intrinsic value.

However, I do regard the effort to apply Nuremberg in detail to the problems that confront us now as a futile undertaking. We must keep in mind the standards to which we committed ourselves there, but I doubt that much is accomplished by describing everything that is going on in Vietnam as criminal in terms of Nuremberg. A more promising path is to examine the policies that we sought to implement in Vietnam and determine whether war is a feasible means of carrying them out.

ROBERT JAY LIFTON: There is little to be gained in discussing which was the greater evil, Auschwitz or Hiroshima. They were both evils, though I think Auschwitz was clearly an expression of a more considered and planned evil and perhaps ultimately a greater one in terms of the individual behavior of those responsible for it; yet Hiroshima, I would insist, retains a very special importance in terms of what it did and what it signifies to us.

I have lived in Tokyo for two or three years at various times in the last fifteen years, and I have also lived and worked in Hiroshima for six months. In Tokyo I never heard people talk with any sense of a continuing awareness of World War II. In Hiroshima I hardly heard anyone talk in a way that didn't convey such awareness.

Anyone who survived the experience of the atomic bomb in Hiroshima, anyone who lived through that one moment in time, then underwent what I think of as a lifelong encounter with death. Life from then on is suffused with the imagery of death. This relates to the fear of after-effect, to the actual occurrence of lethal after-effects such as leukemia, and to a special sense among the survivors of a group identity close to the dead.

The experience of Hiroshima is different from any experience with conventional weapons—not only different in its effect on those who were there, but also in what it signifies for the world. There is with Hiroshima a sense that we have moved beyond limits in destruction, and that is very important. There is a sense that it is now possible to annihilate with totality, to extinguish history through technology.

The fact that the bomb was dropped requires a response from our imagination. Indeed, there is a sense in which the world desperately needs Hiroshima and clings to it. People from all over the world make pilgrimages to Hiroshima and ask the city there for information about it. They want to speak to their own situation, their own fears, in some way by returning to what happened in Hiroshima. I would call that a constructive use of the human imagination—a response appropriate to what actually did occur in Hiroshima and constructive in helping to conserve the human race thereafter.

Finally, I want to speak to the issue of Nuremberg. The trials at Nuremberg did very important things—things to which our imagination can relate and that matter to us now. It also failed on certain counts. But the problem is to use the traditions we have, the places where our imagination can find support from the past, to cope with the unprecedented problems we face now. That means being very critical, and it includes being critical of the professions Telford Taylor mentioned.

It is particularly important for people to be critical within their own professions. When I spoke to a group of physicians about Vietnam, I called my talk "Anti-Healing" and spoke in a polemic way about what I consider an almost criminal conspiracy of silence by physicians. Other things could be said to theologians, lawyers, and, indeed, military men. The purpose is not to condemn but to try to arrive at broader definitions of professional responsibility. Physicians should think of a larger dimension of healing —of really preserving the human race; theologians of a larger, universalistic sense of conscience; and lawyers of a more universal law.

REP. DONALD M. FRASER: I wonder whether it is really useful to define certain conduct as absolutely "criminal" and other conduct as absolutely "legitimate." At least three major factors seem to influence our judgment about the degree of criminality that may be attributed to conduct.

First is the question of utility of conduct. I note that the complaints, previously referred to, of German commanders about the destruction of Balkan towns were predicted on the political consequences for the Germans rather than on the inherent rightness or wrongness of such conduct. In My Lai one can find no utility, and therefore one regards the conduct as essentially wanton.

A second factor is the legitimacy of the objective that brings us into the war. Many of us do not regard American intervention in Vietnam as legitimate, and that undoubtedly influences our attitude toward American conduct there. If, on the other hand, we assume that our objective in Vietnam is legitimate and the other side is pursuing illegimate tactics which threaten to prevent us from reaching that objective, then we are going to be much more willing to resort to questionable conduct.

A third factor would apply to a situation in which we, as a nation, were fighting for survival. In that case, I think, conduct that might have some utility in enabling us to survive would be much less subject to criticism than in either of the other two cases.

RICHARD FALK: The history of the law of war has quite explicitly tried to reconcile considerations of military necessity with the avoidance of unnecessary harm and suffering. In fact, that is the explicit mandate of the law —recognizing the dilemma that one is placed in because some actions that are militarily desirable involve great suffering.

A distinction has been maintained within this broad policy framework between those acts which appear to further belligerent objectives in some way and those which are absolutely prohibited even if they are said to advance military objectives.

One famous illustration of this is the desire of some military commanders during World War II to use poison gas in the Pacific islands. The refusal of the political leaders to endorse the use of gas seemed to be based on moral and legal grounds, not on the fear that the other side would retaliate in kind. There was a situation where we thought we were fighting a legitimate war for a legitimate objective that involved basic interests, yet we acknowledged that part of what we were fighting for was the maintenance of certain standards of limitation on the way in which one employs the instruments of violence.

HANS MORGENTHAU: Congressman Fraser has made a very important point concerning our moral judgment. It is, of course, true that if we regarded the destruction of South Vietnam as an indispensable precondition for our survival, our moral conscience might deplore this necessity, but it would not reject it. In other words, the end justifies the means.

But there are certain absolute principles of prohibition that erect insurmountable obstacles to even those actions that might be justified on pragmatic terms. In the fifteenth and sixteenth centuries, for instance, when virtually anything was allowed in warfare, there was a total ban on the poisoning of wells. This simply was not done; it was a taboo that nobody dared to violate. The Hague Conventions of 1899 and 1907 prohibited the use of dum-dum bullets, which are, under certain conditions, useful but particularly destructive weapons.

We have a tendency today to blame technology for the violation of certain moral principles which, in former times, were regarded to be absolutely binding. But technology is not a self-executing mechanism. It provides certain opportunities for the prospective user, but it does not compel him to take advantage of them.

We have seen in recent history that we have by no means exhausted the technological possibilities of warfare at our disposal. We avoided the use of poison gas in World War II, not for particularly humanitarian reasons, but because it was not feasible. Poison gas is effective in a war of position, such as World War I, but not in a war of movement, because you might poison your own troops, who might move into the region you have poisoned.

One cannot really justify what we are doing in Vietnam on technological grounds. Nor can we expiate our collective guilt by bringing a few individuals to trial. This is psychologically convenient, because once a man has been tried and convicted, we can all say we have recognized the evil that has been done by this man—not by us—in spite of all the instructions to the contrary. Then we can carry on as before, with our consciences relieved.

One cannot get away from the fact that what we are facing here is not primarily a legal problem, domestic or international, or a question of the chain of command. It is the war itself—the kind of war we are waging and the purpose for which we are waging it—which is at fault. And, insofar as the nature of the war is at fault, we are all at fault.

I am convinced that as long as we do not bring this fact home, to ourselves and to the American people, the slogan "No More Vietnams" will be an empty one, or only a tactical one. That is to say, we may not commit another half-million men to the mainland of Asia, we may not subject ourselves again to more than forty thousand casualties, and we may not spend another $30 billion a year for a militarily and politically useless and morally nefarious enterprise. But we will use other tactics, we will fight "clean" Vietnams, where our hands don't get dirty, where we fly in the stratosphere, not seeing what we are hitting and killing.

MARCUS RASKIN: I think it would be useful to pursue two points: to attempt a more careful definition of "war crime" and to determine whether we must rely entirely on international standards, such as those established by the Asian and Nuremberg war crimes trials, or whether there are, in fact, domestic laws that are applicable.

Several references have been made to the implications of our advanced military technology. If we work up to the level of our technology in terms of the wars we are prepared to fight, the sky is the limit: There will be absolutely no control over what the United States can do, because it is the most powerful nation in the world and has the most advanced military technology. Does this mean, then, that no controls at all can be exercised domestically on a runaway military technology? I think we must ask what the United States can do internally to curb its own appetites.

ROBERT JAY LIFTON: We can call it a problem of curbing our appetites or of examining behavior that we haven't really accounted for in international arrangements, especially after World War II. A first step, I think, would be to re-examine Hiroshima. One may concede that the actualities at the end of World War II prevented a full examination; that seems indeed to be a historical truth. But presumably man learns something over the course of his history. If Hiroshima was, as it clearly seems to have been, a kind of quantum leap—from the conventional level of armaments to a level of ultimate technology—then that itself becomes an ethical and legal matter. I don't mean that we can suddenly leave all of our immediate problems with regard to Vietnam, but we must examine them, I think, in connection with a re-evaluation of Hiroshima and nuclear warfare.

REP. DONALD M. FRASER: The point has been made that because both sides engaged in the bombing of civilian populations in World War II, this did not constitute a war crime at the Nuremberg trials.

In Vietnam, tactics of terrorism have been an integral part of the operations of the Vietcong. This is often cited as the justification for our own actions.

Is there some recognized doctrine that suggests that if both sides are doing something wrong, the usual standards need not be brought to bear?

RICHARD FALK: A serious defect of Nuremberg was, in fact, that we were unprepared to have Allied acts appraised by the same standards that were applied to the defeated countries, even though we were at that very moment affirming the opposite principle. We made much of the fact that this was to be a new era of law and restraint in world affairs, yet we exempted ourselves from responsibility of the sort that we were trying to impose on the leaders of defeated countries.

As far as normal attitudes toward criminal responsibility are concerned, it is no defense to allege the fact that comparable acts are being committed by the other side or that one is acting in a criminal way because others have acted in a criminal way.

A limited doctrine of reprisal has developed in international law which has allowed a country to engage in what would be an illegal act in specific retaliation for an illegal act on the part of the other side. This reprisal argument has been invoked by the United States in the Gulf of Tonkin incident and by Israel in the case of the raid against commercial planes in the Beirut airport in December, 1968. But most experts agree that the United Nations

Charter and other international agreements have made it an inappropriate defense to rely on the reprisal doctrine even in specific retaliation for the wrongdoing of others.

There has never been the contention that it was permissible to commit on a retaliatory basis those war crimes which are absolutely prohibited—torture and indiscriminate killing, for example. No government has claimed that it is entitled to torture because the other side is torturing.

TELFORD TAYLOR: It was unquestionably one of the defects in the Nuremberg procedure that it was, so to speak, a one-way street. The tribunal was composed of the victor nations. The jurisdiction was "Axis war crimes." It would have been much better, no doubt, had it been a tribunal of general jurisdiction which could have taken account of activities on both sides.

I believe, however, that under the circumstances existing in 1945, this was impossible. The United Nations was born at the same time. There were no mechanisms available to construct a tribunal of international jurisdiction— at least there didn't seem to be. Therefore, it was done the way it was done.

It was obviously very much harder for a tribunal established by a group of powers that had been conducting large-scale bombing operations to sit there and condemn somebody else for such operations than it would have been for a tribunal of international jurisdiction established on an international basis which could have looked both ways.

If we are to have war crimes trials in the future, it seems to me essential that they should be established under some kind of international auspices so that the jurisdiction applies to both sides.

REP. ABNER J. MIKVA: Were there any instances in the Nuremberg or Tokyo war crimes trials where we condemned conduct as criminal on the part of the Axis even though the Allies had been engaging in the same conduct?

TELFORD TAYLOR: I can't think of any. There was an effort to avoid the invidious situation of condemning general lines of conduct as criminal in which we ourselves had engaged.

There were, no doubt, many cases of isolated war criminal acts by our troops that were not known of or went unpunished. But there were many courts-martial of our own troops for misconduct, and a conscientious effort was made to punish and restrain individuals who violated the rules of war. There was an awareness that these principles should work both ways, which led to the abandonment of the prosecutions on bombing of civilian populations.

RICHARD FALK: The Japanese war crimes trials raised this issue much more directly than the Nuremberg prosecutions did. The first tribunal was constituted by others than the principal Allied powers. One of the judges was an Indian named Pal, and Judge Pal wrote a long dissent to the convictions in which, among other things, he stressed that the defendants were being convicted for crimes that the victors had also perpetrated.

DANIEL ELLISBERG: The doctrine that certain military activities lose their legitimacy when they are carried out by only one side has very interesting implications. In Vietnam we have unique possession of air weapons and such measures as defoliation and herbicides, as well as almost exclusive use of many kinds of arms, vehicles, helicopters, and so forth.

Actually, however, the guiding practice of past war crimes prosecutions has been that crime is something that can only be charged against a loser. Perhaps this explains why successive Presidents have felt so intensely anxious not to lose their war in Vietnam. But whatever happens in Vietnam and whatever it is called—defeat or victory—does not change many important realities in the world. It does not change the power of the United States and it does not change the ability of our American President to avoid being put in the dock by any other nation.

It is also a reality, I think, that no American President will look upon himself as a possible perpetrator of war crimes. It could not occur to him, it could not occur to the American people—except to the young—that war crimes are something that can be charged to Americans.

JONATHAN SCHELL: It does seem that by setting up a court of victors to try criminals selected exclusively from the ranks of the vanquished, we tried at Nuremberg to dissociate ourselves from the people we were convicting, almost to the point, you might say, where we denied our common humanity. Perhaps this allowed us to develop an overly simple view of how war crimes are committed. We did not look closely, for example, at the predicament in which soldiers may find themselves when they are in a situation where brutalization is the rule or where they may be shot for not carrying out certain orders. I don't say this by way of excusing what has happened in Vietnam. But since we did not face these questions at Nuremberg, we are just now discovering these realities and they come to our minds now as excuses for what has happened.

We are left with the question of where to assign responsibility. Some suggest that we must do more than just assign responsibility to the man who actually pulls the trigger. Others contend, with equal justice, that we cast our net too widely if we merely say that all mankind is responsible, that war is hell, and that the My Lai massacre shows that man's nature is fundamentally flawed.

There is very strong motivation for advancing either of these theories, for in either case we can point the finger away from ourselves. In either case the possibility of any kind of effective action is foreclosed.

PHILIP STERN: We need not spend large amounts of time attempting to create a new definition of war crimes. There is a set of rules that we ourselves established at Nuremberg and in the Asian war crime trials. We said certain things were war crimes, and Dr. Falk has quoted Justice Jackson's comment that anything we declared to be a war crime at Nuremberg should apply to American conduct. To what extent have the actions of the United States in Vietnam violated the Nuremberg and Asian war crime precepts?

RICHARD FALK: It seems clear that the basic premise of the Nuremberg judgment was that it was illegal to wage a war of aggression. From that perspective, there is little doubt that the fundamental role of the United States in Vietnam has been an illegal one.

The growth of legal authority within a society takes place by incremental stages. The degree to which domestic law provides us with the basis for proceeding against domestic leaders depends essentially on what it is possible to persuade a political community to do at any particular time. Once society acts, its action becomes a legal precedent. Therefore, the growth of law is a social process that allows a community to articulate those values to which it wants to give its assent and to make those values serve as standards of judgment applicable to individual conduct.

TELFORD TAYLOR: We may be thinking too much in terms of law and trials in approaching this problem. As one who was closely associated with Nuremberg and spent four years involved in that work, I have a fairly high estimate of its importance in the scheme of things. And yet it was a long time ago. Nuremberg is now two quite different things: It is what happened there, and it is also what people think happened there. Perhaps the second is rather more important than the first.

Jonathan Schell observed that perhaps the Nuremberg judges were divorced from reality in that they did not take into account the practical problems confronted by the soldier in combat. Of the many criticisms, I don't think that one is really valid. There were many at Nuremberg who had been involved in the war recently, and anyhow Nuremberg was not primarily concerned with what happened on the battlefield.

Most of what was involved in the trials was quite remote from the scene of actual combat and did not concern the acts of soldiers. It concerned, for the most part, the higher-ranking people to whom Mr. Ellsberg referred. The prosecution was helped by the fact that the Germans were very good record keepers, so that most of the orders which had been given for the conduct charged as criminal were carefully preserved. A very large part of the trials could, therefore, be conducted on a documentary basis involving the people who actually gave the orders.

There is much misunderstanding about this doctrine of superior orders. It does serve to widen the responsibility beyond the "trigger man," and the effect of it is not to eliminate responsibility, but to move it upward. If the responsibility rests with the person who gave the order, that is where the criminal sanction should be applied.

One other point: I have heard it said that Nuremberg established the sort of thing that Americans don't do, and that it has, therefore, come as a shock to find that they are doing just those things today. I think that anyone who was at Nuremberg would have come away with exactly the opposite impression. Any notion that the crimes tried at Nuremberg were committed because Germans are Germans, or anything like that, was quite exploded by prolonged contact with the situation. One became aware that most of these things had been done by very ordinary men and women, that their crimes were the product not of some intrinsic viciousness or bestiality as individuals but of the environment they were in, the climate of opinion that had become acceptable, the policies that were being carried out. It was, allowing for some exceptions, not at all a matter of individual depravity. The Nuremberg offenses could be committed by ordinary people, and Americans for the most part are ordinary people.

This brings me back to the question of what ought to be done. To discuss this entirely in terms of whether we should have more trials, whether we should try ourselves, whether we should impose criminal liability on our leaders, seems to me to be talking about solutions that are interesting conceptually but not very realistic.

REP. ROBERT W. KASTENMEIER: In the long sweep of history, most governments find it quite difficult to make dispassionate judgments on their own conduct in the course of war. Nuremberg, of course, was a case of the victors applying standards to the vanquished.

Apart from what we might do internally at this time in the United States, does the United Nations or any other international agency provide the possibility of a constructive role in assessing accountability for some of the abuses that have taken place since World War II?

TELFORD TAYLOR: The question is susceptible to a great variety of answers. My own feeling is that the international agencies likely to be available for this purpose are generally restricted to such objectives as informal consideration and education.

There is, of course, the Court of Human Rights in Strasbourg. There are other such agencies. But they are all of limited jurisdiction, and they have had very little business. The likelihood of the United Nations establishing some kind of meaningful international criminal jurisdiction seems, at the moment, rather remote.

In the years since Nuremberg, quite a few efforts have been made to codify the laws of war through the International War Commission and other agencies. By and large, these have been halting efforts and not very fruitful. I don't mean to denigrate them completely, but I am afraid my feeling is, at this time, one of limited confidence in the creation of international bodies that could operate in a very meaningful way.

REP. DON EDWARDS: A group of Congressmen recently visited the World Court at the Hague, and the judges were so delighted to have visitors that they stopped everything. They did not have anything to do. One case has been referred to the World Court in the last five or six years— and it was not referred by the United States.

International law, like domestic law, must have the consent and the good intentions of the people or the governments that are subject to it. We have that problem in the United States, and we have it to a much greater extent with regard to the World Court and other international organizations.

RICHARD FALK: One very positive step that could be taken at this point would be the convening of a world conference of governments. Two principal purposes would be served by such a conference. It could bring up to date the rules of war, which have undergone no fundamental revision since 1899 and are now very obsolete.

The second—and more important—purpose of a world conference would be essentially political. The very process of convening and participating in such a conference would promote an awareness of the war crimes issue at the highest levels of governments. Such an effort, if it succeeded, would lend new emphasis to the obligations of restraint and allow new pressure to be brought to bear internally on the formulation of policy.

REP. HENRY S. REUSS: I can see some utility in the creation of two different commissions to deal with various aspects of the problem of war crimes. The first would be a commission of jurists—American jurists because we are Americans—to make recommendations on a number of legal, juridical matters, including these:

First, the application of existing facets of the law of war to some of the hellishness that has been brought to our attention in Vietnam;

Second, the development of a body of law, national and international, to deal with the long-term environmental assaults that seem to be a byproduct of modern war;

Third, a post-Nuremberg attempt to set forth new principles of law, national and international, to fill gaps in the existing codes;

Fourth, the development of legal instrumentalities, courts and tribunals.

The second commission that I think would be useful would address itself to violations of international legal and moral standards today, with particular reference to Vietnam. This commission could offer a forum to those returning soldiers and others who have something to say but who now have no recourse to existing bodies, including the regular committees of Congress.

I am not quite sure whether such a commission should be made up of distinguished citizens who are not officials, or whether it should be composed of the twenty or so Senators and Representatives whose names readily come to mind as persons interested in this subject and able to provide protection against reprisals for those who choose to give it evidence. Perhaps the commission should be composed of both legislators and private citizens.

I do believe there is a need for such a forum. The Con-

gress, which has organizational and seniority troubles of
its own, has not assumed this responsibility, nor is its leadership disposed to interfere with those committees which
ought to be doing something about it but are not.

BENJAMIN V. COHEN: In our anxiety to deal with this
matter of war crimes, we tend to make the same mistake
in the international field that we are now making in this
country in the domestic field: We direct too much of our
attention to the problem of trial and punishments, rather
than to the causes and prevention of these crimes and
tragedies. By addressing ourselves to cause and prevention, we have an opportunity to unite our public opinion
together rather than to divide it. We cannot condone the
commission of war crimes and must punish the guilty; but
we must temper justice with mercy, remembering that the
whole nation bears a responsibility for letting our armed
forces become involved in a civil war in a foreign land
where civilians are participants and atrocities are likely to
occur.

REP. JONATHAN BINGHAM: I heartily agree with Dr. Cohen. It would be a mistake for us to put all military activities in Vietnam or all use of violence in one basket, so to
speak, and say that it is all part of one tremendous evil and
that there are no distinctions to be made. If one believes
that majority opinion in this country does not regard the
entire Vietnam effort as an evil, illegal, and criminal effort,
then one must draw a distinction between the various
types of activities that have been carried on—to distinguish, for example, between My Lai, on the one hand, and
the use of the free-fire zone on the other. As far as I have
been able to determine, the kind of thing that happened
at My Lai was clearly in violation of all Government and
military policy.

Material furnished by the Department of Defense indicates that, at least in principle, a conscientious effort is made to instruct our military personnel about their obligations under the Geneva Convention: that it is their obligation to disobey an unlawful order, that they can be punished as war criminals if they violate the provisions of the Geneva Convention, and that it is no defense in such a prosecution that they may have been given an unlawful order.

In the case of My Lai, therefore, I don't believe it can be argued that American policy was the crime. On the other hand, the kind of thing that takes place in the free-fire zones, when aircraft are instructed to attack villages and kill the inhabitants, is quite a different proposition. There, I would say, the policy is the crime. We must make these distinctions and condemn those policies—defoliation, indiscriminate bombing—without insisting that every individual crime committed in the war is a reflection of "criminal" American policy.

PHILIP NOEL-BAKER: I should like to comment, from personal experience, on the restraining power of the laws of war. Before 1914, I studied international law at Cambridge. I knew of the work of the two Hague Conferences. As a British Member of Parliament, my father had led a delegation to the Hague in 1907 to demand world compulsory arbitration of international disputes and a halt to the arms race then gathering momentum.

I was at Ypres when the first gas attack of World War I occurred. I remember the horror of watching Canadian soldiers die with yellow froth oozing from their mouths. I remember the passionate anger that went around the world that the Hague Code had been breached. It was to be breached many more times.

I remember that before the end of the war the Bavarians, whom I had loved in peacetime, killed their prisoners because they were notoriously cruel in war, and I remember how a British Highland regiment, in which I had a cousin serving, killed its prisoners in reprisal.

When the war was over, I went straight into the League of Nations Section of the Foreign Office and I became a close friend of the head of that section, Sir Cecil Hurst, who later became president of the permanent Court of International justice. I said to Hurst: "Do you really think that in helping to draft the laws of war, in helping to draft the Declaration of London in 1909 about naval warfare and the use of the submarine, you were creating a better atmosphere? Do you think you were helping to promote peace or to humanize war when it came? Would you not have done better to concentrate attention on the international court, international arbitration, and the stopping of the arms race?" And he said, "Yes, we would have."

I believe the malignant spiral of the decline of the laws of war as a restraint on violence is still inevitable. Between 1919 and 1939, great efforts were made to restore the binding power of the laws of war: the Geneva Protocol of 1925 on chemical and biological warfare; the clauses of Anthony Eden's draft disarmament treaty of 1933, which declared illegal the use of fire. Bombing from the air and unrestricted submarine warfare were always illegal under the established precepts of international law. When Hitler bombed Guernica with fire bombs in 1937, a new passion of anger swept the world. But thirteen years later Seoul was burnt to the ground when the North Korean forces advanced, and was burnt to the ground in the name of the United Nations. In Vietnam the U.S. forces started from the acceptability of air bombing by B-52s, from the acceptability of napalm, and they came by a pretty rapid process to the use of chemical agents.

On February 2, 1970, my Labor Government made a written answer in the House of Commons—a written answer so that they could not be attacked by supplementary oral questions—which said that the use of CS gas and "such other gases"—meaning, of course, the herbicides and defoliants—were outside the scope of the Geneva Protocol of 1925. I can give personal evidence on that matter. I had many friends who took part in that conference. One of them, Henri Bonnet, still remembered in Washington as a great French Ambassador after 1945, told me, "Yes, the formula does forbid every kind of chemical and biological weapon that can be conceived now or in the future. And rightly, because some day, some criminal lunatic might think of inventing a gas that would destroy animals or crops." That seemed unthinkably wicked in 1925.

In 1930, when the issue of tear gas was raised, I took part in drafting the documents which Robert Cecil laid before the Preparatory Commission of the Disarmament Conference, which declared that every gas, including every kind of tear gas, was banned by the Geneva Protocol of 1925. I was there at the Disarmament Conference when Eden's "established rules of international law" were constantly discussed and universally upheld.

If I am now asked whether it would be desirable to try to revive the binding power of the laws of war, to have a government conference, to draw up a new code, I would have to answer that I won't oppose it, provided that it does not divert attention from what really matters. I think the laws of war have done a great deal of good since Grotius first tried to write them. Even in the 1914 and 1939 wars they helped prisoners of war and civilians. But the real issue is that of aggression. I believe that if you concentrate too much on the laws of war you divert attention from the prevention of all wars. You can't isolate Vietnam. It is part of the general problem of restoring the sanctity of the United Nations Charter, which categorically forbids all use of force in international disputes, except by authority of the United Nations. This outlawing of war is still our best hope. Let no one say this is blind idealism. The idealists, the romanticists, the illusionists are those who tell us that armaments can give us safety, peace, and order.

The only realism today is to secure the abolition of armaments and war. It is the armaments themselves which create the dangers against which they are supposed to guard. A supreme effort to root out militarism from the governments' thinking must be made. The hour is late, but it can still be done.

LOUIS POLLAK: I would urge that we eschew overlegalization of the issues and recognize them for what they are —political issues, for which we as citizens have responsibility. I see little profit, for example, in exploring the question of whether our military participation in Vietnam is legal or illegal. Similarly, I have no great enthusiasm for exploring questions of whether SEATO and comparable arrangements are or are not compatible with the United Nations Charter, or whether these arrangements are in other respects in conformity with our obligations under international or domestic law.

To devote too much attention to the legal questions becomes an escape device that diverts us from our aggregate responsibilities as citizens, whether or not we happen to have the disadvantage of being lawyers.

The question of the legality of our involvement in Vietnam will serve as an example. The fact that we are engaged in an enormous armed conflict which has never been declared by Congress does not mean that it is an illegal war; or, if it does mean that, the label "illegal" becomes a triviality. We have spent a vast part of our history engaged in military operations for which no war was declared but in which the President of the United States has employed his authority as Commander-in-Chief with various forms of acquiescence from Congress. With respect to this current venture, the forms of Congressional support, be they a Tonkin Gulf Resolution or repeated appropriations, are at every hand.

I don't mean to suggest that it is irrelevant whether or not Congress assumes the responsibility of declaring war. I think its failure to do so is a form of abdication, and it would at least be better manners if our Congress would do themselves—and ourselves and our enemies and possibly even our allies—the justice of declaring war when that is the business we are engaged in. But to talk about it as a legal problem seems to me to trivialize our history and our notions about law.

I would make the same point about some of the less inflammatory questions of the legality of one or another of our international security arrangements. Are they in conformity with various overriding obligations of international law, including the United Nations Charter? These are not questions that mean much in the abstract. The answers depend very much on what we are doing in particular situations.

I was one of those who felt that we were right under President Truman to send troops into Korea. I thought so then and I think so now. Various views have been expressed about the legality of that undertaking, and the matter is still being debated. But I would be much more interested in pursuing a debate on whether it was responsible politics in the highest sense of that word, on whether it was proper international policy. That was my view about the Korean intervention.

I happen to have a very different view about our role in Vietnam. I would say that it is tragic and very bad policy. I don't need to weigh that down by also urging that it is illegal; if I thought it legal, it would not make it better policy.

The second but closely related reason for my urging that we not overlegalize these problems is that they are not problems that lend themselves to resolution by a tribunal. The writ of law runs to particular problems, particular activities, and particular people. It does not run to enjoin hunger or poverty or racial discrimination, and it certainly does not run to enjoin war. I think it would be a perversion of institutions that have difficult but limited roles to play if the courts were to enter that kind of undertaking.

That does not mean that there are no useful roles for courts to play. Were there American courts in Vietnam other than military courts, they could try as murder the offenses alleged at My Lai—and if those offenses took place, murders they surely were.

I don't find it very useful to talk about those alleged offenses as genocide. We have nothing that indicates that the definition of that offense has been met. The offenses in Vietnam do not seem to have been as eloquent, if I may put it rather grimly, as that. They would appear to have been offenses against people who were not regarded as human at all, rather than against people whom there was an attempt to destroy in whole or in part. I doubt if we have crimes of genocide, but undoubtedly we have crimes of murder and violations of the rules of war which are treatable by courts. And we do have a gap in our judicial structure.

As things stand now, there are no national courts which can do business abroad. We have had such courts at other times in our history, and if we are going to maintain a massive presence abroad for a long period of time, we should look to re-establishing them.

What I have been saying is not meant to suggest that I regard it as unimportant to pursue, as a major part of our national objectives, the systematic development of endorsable norms of international law. There has been an unfortunate trend in the opposite direction. One sign of deterioration within this last decade has been the decline in stature of the International Court of Justice, which now has no cases on its docket.

We should take a more enthusiastic interest in the United Nations than we have in recent Administrations, Republican and Democratic. We must continue to pursue treaty arrangements which look to the upgrading of international legal conduct and of those activities of domestic conduct which clearly have implications for international peace and well-being. The movement in international law is a slow one, but it can move if we are purposeful about it.

But we must remember that the pressing issues before us are not, by being talked about as legal issues, stripped of their central political meaning. We must not lose responsibility for addressing ourselves to them by talking about them in legal terms.

HANNAH ARENDT: I know that the war in Vietnam is not the first and will not be the last undeclared war. But I think Dean Pollak overlooked an important point: When a nation declares war, it implies that it is prepared to play the game according to the rules. Since the beginning of this century there have been attempts to lay down certain laws for war. By not declaring war, a nation manages to evade even these feeble limitations.

PRISCILLA HOLMES: I think the rules of law do serve a very useful purpose: They help form public opinion and provide a basis for individual judgments of one's own and others' conduct. In the terrible confusion about Vietnam, the existence of a recognized body of law could provide an important beginning toward the achievement of a new national consensus.

REP. WILLIAM F. RYAN: I am concerned about the apparent de-emphasis on law throughout the course of our discussions. I would urge against any such de-emphasis.

It was suggested by Dean Pollak that we ought to eschew the legal question and look at Vietnam as a political question. It seems to me the legal profession has a particular obligation to raise the Constitutional issue at every opportunity. The Constitution still says, "Congress shall have power to declare war."

At the least, our laws should reflect our morality. To be sure, in some cases the felt tradition of a society is less than enlightened. In those instances, our laws should be in the vanguard, working to create a consensus for the enlightened views they embody although these may not yet be fully subscribed to by the public. In brief, our laws are the constructs which encompass our morality and which, when necessary, transmute it into a more enlightened form.

If we conclude, as I do, that morality has been violated by the Vietnam war and by My Lai, then we are compelled to raise some essential questions about the system of law which, we maintain, supports our democratic Government and enables it to respond to the needs of the people.

First, we must ask whether our laws and our morality are out of joint—do our laws vouchsafe this war, while morality condemns it? Second, we must ask how, if this first question is answered in the affirmative, our laws should be changed. Third, we must ask whether, if our own internal laws are not violated, international law is transgressed.

I think we, as Congressmen, are obliged to carry our case to the people on these questions. Not only is it our responsibility, as elected leaders, to express our conception of morality; we are even more compelled, as men and women sworn to uphold the Constitution, to stress our responsibility for the legality of what this nation does.

I believe that this war does, in a most elemental sense, violate our own internal law. Our basic law need not, I think, be changed, since it marks this war as illegal. But our laws must be followed.

Let me briefly explain my conclusion that our present law is violated by the Vietnam war. It may be cant to some to recite the Constitution's provision in Article I, Section 8, that it is Congress' power to declare war, but it is fact that these words remain incontrovertible. It is our responsibility as Congressmen constantly to invoke these words, lest we acknowledge that they have been amended out of the Constitution by virtue of Congressional default to Executive dictate.

Since the declaration of war is a responsibility of Congress—probably the most important responsibility it has—and since we are, to state the obvious, embroiled in an armed conflict, the conclusion seems clear that there has been a failure to adhere to the Constitution. This flaw lies not in our law, but in the Executive's failure to obey it and the failure of Congress to enforce it. And, ultimately, the responsibility for this flaw extends beyond the Government to all the people, since it is they who choose the Executive and elect the Congress.

Once this failure of obedience to the law and this failure to resist that disobedience are recognized, the intimate connection with our perception of the My Lai massacre is seen. My Lai reflects a breakdown of law, much as does the war. Condemnation of the former implicitly corresponds to condemnation of the latter.

I think my point is clear. Law is a very real and very viable consideration in our concern for ending the war in Vietnam, for foreclosing the possibility of future Vietnams, and for condemning the My Lai massacre and preventing such events in the future.

I would add that an emphasis on law implicitly upholds the belief that the procedures by which laws are enacted, implemented, and enforced are to be fair and responsible. Thus, if we in Congress are to protect the right of dissent, oppose secrecy, deal with the question of selective conscientious objection—if we are really going to act as Congressmen should act—we ourselves must confront the system that has made it possible for committee barons to run the Congress and frustrate the will of the people. We simply can no longer support a system that puts in places of high power people who have not only advocated this war but have been its principal architects.

II

TECHNOLOGY AND AMERICAN POWER:

The Changing Nature of War

"After the end of World War II, and as a result of the Nuremberg trials, we justly condemned the willful destruction of an entire people and its culture, calling this crime against humanity *genocide.* It seems to me that the willful and permanent destruction of environment in which a people can live in a manner of their own choosing ought similarly to be considered as a crime against humanity, to be designated by the term *ecocide.*"
—ARTHUR W. GALSTON

GABRIEL KOLKO: There are no census takers of the barbarism of the twentieth century, and there has been far too much of it to measure. The executioners are not willing and the victims are rarely able to provide exact details. What is certain in Vietnam, save to those who have neither the will nor the interest to confront truth, is the general magnitude and quality of the United States' combat against the Vietnamese. This relationship has a logic and structure which leads to war crimes as the inevitable consequence of a war that is intrinsically criminal. More important, the war is the outcome of America's post–World War II foreign policy and its effort to relate its industrial power to the political and ideological realities of popular revolutionary movements in the Third World.

After World War II the United States pursued its diplomacy on the traditional postulate of military power ultimately being based on physical plant, economic capacity, and the ability to destroy it. This assumption was also a definition of the nature of the world conflict, which prior to 1950 had always been between industrial nations, and after 1945 designated the Soviet Union as the primary threat to American security and interests. Such a premise, which not so much discounted as ignored the mobilizing potential of ideology and the capability of Third World guerrilla and liberation movements, gave the United States supreme confidence in the efficacy and strategic doctrines of its own military. This armed force was designed essentially to operate against a centralized, industrial society, a reinforcing proposition Washington thought warranted by the military and diplomatic facts, as well as by its own economic priorities. Every strategy has a price tag, and strategic bombing has a predictable and relatively low cost, but it also necessitated a convenient and vulnerable industrial enemy.

The Korean war, which almost resulted in an American defeat, shattered a half-century of conventional wisdom and raised a critical dilemma. It immediately proved the limits of existing military strategy and technology against decentralized, nonindustrial nations. Apart from political or humanitarian considerations, there were no decisive targets against which to employ the atomic military technology on which the United States had pinned the bulk of its hopes and money.

After weakening its power everywhere else in the world and embarking on what was to become the second most expensive war in its history, the United States waged the Korean war with "conventional" arms intended for combat between industrial nations. Fought against comparatively poorly armed peasants, it was a war unlike any in modern history, and the Korean precedent reveals the principles and tactics to emerge in Vietnam in a more intensive form. Within three months the United States destroyed all usual strategic targets in North Korea, and over the last two years of the war it dropped about six times the tonnage used during the first year. Camps for noncombatants contained over 400,000 persons under guard, one-eighth of whom died of disease and starvation. Half the South Korean population was homeless or refugees by early 1951; 2.5 million were refugees at war's end; twice that number were on relief; over one million South Korean civilians died; and estimates of North Korea's losses are still greater. As Major General Emmett O'Donnell, Jr., head of the Far Eastern Bomber Command, reported to the Senate in mid-1951: "I would say that the entire Korean Peninsula is just a terrible mess. Everything is destroyed. There is nothing standing worthy of the name." The Korean war, in brief, became a war against an entire nation, civilians and soldiers, Communists and anti-Communists alike, with everything regarded as a legitimate target for attack. By 1953, when the United States was further from military victory or mastery than in the fall of 1950, the most important undamaged targets were the twenty irrigation dams so vital to the rice crop and civilian population of the North. Restraints operated until mid-May, 1953, when five of these dams were destroyed, in one instance resulting in a flash flood that scooped clean twenty-seven miles of valley.

For the Koreans, the war's magnitude led to vast human suffering, but the United States learned that it was unable to translate its immense firepower into military or political victory for itself or its allies. There was, in brief, no conceivable relationship between the expenditure of arms and the political or military results obtained. As the official Army history relates, utilizing high mobility, decentralization, and tunnel defenses, the North Korean and Chinese armies greatly improved their equipment and logistics and ended the war "a formidable foe who bore little resemblance to the feeble nation of World War II." Massive firepower had resulted in enormous civilian casualties and barbarism, but inhumanity was not victory.

The implications of Korea to the future of the United States were monumental, conjuring up the prospect of political and military defeat in Asia and vividly revealing the limits of its power. Massive land armies were both very expensive and of dubious utility, and it was in this context that John Foster Dulles attempted to break through the enigma with his "massive retaliation" debate—never satisfactorily translating it into a coherent strategy. Not only did Soviet nuclear power rule out attacking Russia with impunity, but even Washington doubted in the spring of 1954 whether Vietnamese peasants could be made to stop fighting if Moscow were destroyed, and the debate over employing atomic bombs at Dien Bien Phu only revealed that in close combat and mixed battle lines atomic bombs indiscriminately destroy friend and foe alike.

The dilemma of relating American technology to agrarian and decentralized societies had not been resolved by the time President Kennedy came to office. Without delving into the "counterinsurgency" planning and assumptions which the President immediately authorized General Maxwell D. Taylor to coordinate and study, it is sufficient to observe that when the United States began making its commitments in Vietnam, it was keenly aware of the failures of the past, but was still en-

cumbered by the same limitations which might only repeat the Korean precedent of mass firepower, wholesale
destruction of populations, and political-military failure.
Nor is it necessary to review the familiar history of how
the Kennedy and Johnson Administrations intensified
their involvement in Vietnam. More relevant is the distinctive character of that war and the assumptions and
manner in which the United States has employed its military might. I propose to outline the political and environmental structure of the war and to show why the United
States consciously employs a technology that is quantita-
tively far greater than that used in Korea but inevitably
requires the same outcome in Vietnam—the destruction
of untold masses of people and their society and the moral
immunization of the American civilians and soldiers
called upon to sustain and implement the Government's
grand strategy.

  One of the most significant realities of the war in Vietnam, a fact which makes "legal" combat impossible and
necessitates endless crimes against civilians and combatants alike, is the absence of conventional military fronts
and areas of uncontested American control. The Tet
offensive of 1968 proved once again that combat can occur anywhere and that the military initiative rests with
the National Liberation Front. American forces, in reality,
form enclaves in a sea of hostility and instability, able
temporarily to contest N.L.F. physical control over large
regions but incapable of establishing durable control by
winning the political and ideological loyalties of the large
majority of the people. Perhaps most ironically, the N.L.F.
has been able to transform this American presence, which
it has not been able to remove physically, into a symbiotic
relationship from which they extract maximum possible
assets in what is intrinsically an intolerable and undesired
situation. For this reason as well, they are able to endure

the war the longest, prevail, and win at the end, even should they lose a great number of military encounters.

The Pentagon's statements notwithstanding, there now exists more than sufficient documentation proving that United States' claims to "control" 67 per cent of the South Vietnamese population as of before Tet 1968 or 92 per cent as of late 1969 bear no relationship to reality. Suffice it to say, the Pentagon also maintains private figures—data that simply reinforce the inescapable conclusions of a logical analysis of its own releases—that a very substantial majority of the South Vietnamese are not under the physical "control" of either the Saigon regime or American forces. The supreme irony of the war in Vietnam is that hamlets labeled "secure" for public purposes are often the hardest hit by American arms. The reason is fundamental: Areas, villages, and large population concentrations under the operational control of the N.L.F. frequently cooperate in Saigon-sponsored surveys and projects to spare themselves unnecessary conflict with American and Saigon forces. To lie about the presence of the N.L.F. to a visiting pacification officer is a small matter in comparison to the certain military consequences the truth will invite. What the Pentagon describes as the "secure" area in Vietnam is often a staging and economic base as secure and vital to the N.L.F. as its explicitly identified liberated zones.

Therefore, we read innumerable accounts of trade and movement between Saigon-"controlled" areas and those of the N.L.F. and of "friendly" villagers and Saigon's Popular Forces (only one-eighth of whom are trusted with arms) who fail to report N.L.F. combat units and infrastructures. Hence, too, the existence of at least five thousand N.L.F. political workers in the greater Saigon area, to use minimal American figures, and the undoubted accuracy of the N.L.F. claim to have parallel governments in all the major cities and towns. American admissions that three-quarters of the N.L.F. budget in 1968 was raised from taxes collected from one-half the Vietnamese population, that Saigon's eight largest corporations paid an average of $100,000 each in taxes to the N.L.F., or that it purchases vast quantities of supplies from "secure" towns are much more to the point. To some critical measure, "secure" areas are both a part of, and vital to, the N.L.F. And to be "secure" is not to be a continuous free-fire zone. The question is not who claims "control" but who really possesses it. For the most part, such control as the United States may have is temporary, and ultimately is based on its ability and willingness to apply firepower, and certainly is not a consequence of any popular support for its universally corrupt regime in Saigon.

The refugee camps and program are good examples of the N.L.F.'s ability to turn what the United States intends as adversity into a dual-edged institution from which the N.L.F. may gain as much as a repressive situation allows —so long as it retains the respect and political loyalty of the people. These camps were the inevitable byproduct of America's massive firepower applied to all Vietnam and its explicit desire to reconcentrate the population so as to better control it. "You have to be able to separate the sheep from the goats," one Pentagon-sponsored analyst said in 1966. "The way to do it is harsh. You would have to put all military-age males in the army or in camps as you pacify the country. Anyone not in the army or in a camp is a target. He's either a Vietcong or is helping them."

By May, 1969, the war had produced 3,153,000 refugees since 1965, 612,000 still remaining in camps and only a tiny fraction having been resettled in their original villages. The large majority of the refugees, as every objective account agrees, were seeking to escape the free-fire zones and the rain of fire the Americans were showering on them. Their political loyalties were anti-Saigon in the

large majority of cases, and the intense squalor, degradation, and corruption in the camps undoubtedly mitigated
such small sympathy for the anti-N.L.F. cause as may exist.
No less significant is the very high percentage of old men,
women, and children—that is, noncombatants—in the
camps. In this sense, refugees escape the American bombs
by entering the American camps, while the younger men
generally remain in the combat areas. Roger Hilsman put
it another way in 1967: "I think it would be a mistake to
think that the refugees come toward the Government side
out of sympathy. . . . [They] come toward the Government
side simply because the Vietcong do not bomb, and that
they will not at least be bombed and shelled. I have
greater worries that some of the refugee camps are rest
areas for the Vietcong, precisely because of this."

Refugee camps therefore become incubators of opposition as well as potential shelters for it, just as many reported N.L.F. defectors, very few of whom are regular
combatants, are now suspected of returning to N.L.F.
ranks after a period of recuperation. This integration of
the institutional structure of "secure" areas with that
dominated by N.L.F., this profound lack of clear lines and
commitments among the Vietnamese, attains its ultimate
danger for the Americans when it is revealed that the
Vietnamese support for the N.L.F. extends to parts of the
highest levels of the Saigon regime. We know little of the
process by which Vu Ngoc Nha, Huynh Van Trong, and
their thirty-nine associates penetrated the intimate circle
of the Thieu regime and became privy to its secrets, but
it is certain that many officers, soldiers, and administrators
of the Saigon regime are secretly committed to the N.L.F.
cause, and it is no less certain that most other Saigon
leaders are deeply dedicated to enriching themselves,
even through trade with the N.L.F. regions, and are totally
unreliable for the ultimate purposes of the United States.
Such an army of unwilling conscripts, corrupt officers, and

politically unreliable elements in their midst is a dubious asset to the United States and alone scarcely an unmanageable threat to the N.L.F. Hence the chimera of "Vietnamization." The various Administrations have known all this and much more.

It is one of the lessons of twentieth-century history that repression and social disintegration generate forces of opposition that otherwise would not have existed, and Vietnam is no exception. No one can comprehend the development and success of the N.L.F. without appreciating this fact. Vietnamese forced out of their villages by air and artillery strikes and into decrepit and unsanitary camps know full well that the Americans are responsible. The army of prostitutes are aware of the source of their degradation. The peasant whose crops are defoliated knows whom to blame. Apart from its attractive political program and land reform policy, the N.L.F. has successfully capitalized on the almost universal Vietnamese hatred of foreign invaders, a fact that has made its political infrastructure and loyalties of the people to it increasingly durable even as growing firepower is inflicted upon them. "They say this village is 80 per cent VC supporters," one American officer commented in September, 1969, as his men combed a village. "By the time we finish this, it will be 95 per cent." Such insight is scarcely atypical, but appears to be universal in the available documents on this aspect of the war.

This realism on repression intensifying resistance, as well as every other phase of the struggle in Vietnam I have mentioned, sets the indispensable context in which the United States applies its military power, for it long ago stopped operating within the acknowledged political limits of South Vietnam. More precisely, by employing sheer physical might, the United States has sought to compensate for and transcend its unavoidable political weaknesses in its Vietnam adventure. The various men in the

White House and Pentagon know better than any of us that the lines are indeed everywhere and that the Vietnamese people are overwhelmingly real and potential enemies. And since the Vietnamese long ceased to be promising ideological targets, tractable to successive corrupt regimes, they have virtually all become physical targets everywhere. Quite apart from the results—for the United States is slowly learning that its efforts have become both militarily insufficient and politically self-defeating—the necessary logic of American military strategy in Vietnam is to wage war against the entire Vietnamese people, men, women, and children alike, wherever they may be found. So long as it remains in Vietnam, it cannot fight another kind of war with any hope of success.

The original theory of counterinsurgency in White House circles in 1961 was that a limited number of men, wise in the ways of guerrilla ideology and tactics, could enter the jungles with conventional small arms and win. Given the political, military, and ideological realities, this premise was utterly discredited by 1964, and there followed a major scramble to develop new "miracle" weapons intended to overcome the N.L.F.'s clear military superiority. The problem, however, is that it requires five to seven years to translate a sophisticated weapons concept into adequate field deployment, and in 1965 weapons ideas already in progress were designed overwhelmingly for a war in Europe. A mass of exotic crash research proposals proved, on the whole, to be expensive miscarriages, but projects already commissioned in helicopters and gunships seemed most readily transferable to the Vietnam context. The helicopter's distinctive value pointed to the defining objective condition of the military phase of the Vietnam war: decentralization and a lack of military targets. Without the mobility the helicopter provided, General William C. Westmoreland has estimated, one million more troops would have been required to fight the same war on the ground.

While the United States has sought to discover and procure weapons uniquely designed for the decentralized agrarian and jungle environment, it has also attempted to use existing weapons first designed for such concentrated strategic targets as industry and air-missile bases. This, by necessity, has required employing weapons such as the B-52, originally constructed for intensive, nuclear warfare against stationary targets. It has adjusted for decentralized mobile targets simply by dropping much greater quantities of explosives of immense yield on vast regions with very few permanent military installations. Militarily, the United States has therefore fought the war with whatever decentralized-style weapons it could develop as well as with the sheer quantity of firepower which "conventional" weapons employ. The preeminent characteristic of both these approaches is that they are intrinsically utterly indiscriminate—they strike entire populations. While such strategy violates all international law regarding warfare and is inherently genocidal, it also adjusts to the political reality in South Vietnam that the N.L.F. is and can be anywhere and that virtually the entire people is America's enemy.

I am not contriving something the Pentagon does not already know. "The unparalleled, lavish use of firepower as a substitute for manpower," writes one of its analysts in an official publication, "is an outstanding characteristic of U.S. military tactics in the Vietnam war." From 315,000 tons of air ordnance dropped in Southeast Asia in 1965, the quantity by January–October, 1969, the peak year of the war, reached 1,388,000 tons. Over that period, 4,580,000 tons were dropped on Southeast Asia, or six and one-half times that employed in Korea. To this we must add ground munitions, which rose from 577,000 tons in 1966 to 1,278,000 tons in the first eleven months of 1969.

And to these destruction-intensive weapons applied extensively we must also add the wide-impact decentralized weapons that are employed in ever greater quantities alone or in conjunction with traditional explosives. For the family of cluster bomb weapons and flechette rockets, which the Air Force rates as "highly successful," I have no procurement data. Suffice it to say, these are exclusively anti-personnel weapons covering much wider areas than bombs. Procurement of CS (a type of advanced tear gas) went up twenty-four times from 1965 to 1969. Procurement of defoliants and anti-crop chemicals is erratic because of inventory and production problems, though the Air Force's far too conservative data on acreage sprayed has risen quite consistently from less than 100,000 acres in 1964 to an adjusted annual rate of fifteen times as high in 1969. Procurement was $1.7 million in 1964 and $15.9 million in 1970, with an inventory in 1970 almost equal to new purchases.

Translated into human terms, the United States has made South Vietnam a sea of fire as a matter of policy, turning an entire nation into a target. This is not accidental but intentional and intrinsic to the strategic and political premises of the Vietnam war. By necessity it destroys villages, slaughters all who are in the way, uproots families, and shatters a whole society. There is a mountain of illustrations, but let me take only one here—that of the B-52—which reveals how totally conscious this strategy is.

The B-52s cost about $850 million to operate in Southeast Asia in fiscal 1970, a bit less than 1969 but far more than 1968, and they dropped about 43,000 tons a month. On what? The one official survey of actual hits that I have been able to locate states that "enemy camps," often villages full of civilians, "were where intelligence said they would be" in only one-half the cases. In "the other half, intelligence was faulty,and the camps were either not there or the VC had not been in the target area when the bombs fell." Then on whom did the bombs fall? On Vietnamese peasants in both cases, on thousands of My Lais.

Stated another way, in 1968 and 1969 the United States used about 7,700 to 7,800 tons of ground and air ordnance during an average day. At the time of the 1968 Tet offensive, the Pentagon estimates, N.L.F. forces were consuming a peak of twenty-seven tons of ammunition a day, and half that amount during an average day in April, 1969. Roughly, this is a ratio of 250 or 500 to one. Inequalities of similar magnitude appear when one compares overall supply, including food, which for all N.L.F. and North Vietnamese forces in the south was 7,500 tons per month at the end of 1968. At the beginning of 1968, American fuel needs alone were 14 million tons a month. Out of this staggering ratio of conspicuous consumption has come not only conspicuous failure for the United States, but also a level of firepower that so far exceeds distinctions between combatants and noncombatants as to be necessarily aimed at all Vietnamese.

In an air and mechanical war against an entire people, in which no fixed lines exist and high mobility and decentralization give the N.L.F. a decisive military advantage, barbarism can be the only consequence of American sledgehammer tactics. During Tet 1968, when the United States learned that the "secure" areas can become part of the front when the N.L.F. so chooses, U.S. air and artillery strikes destroyed half of Mytho, with a population of 70,-000, four-fifths of Hue's inner city, and more than one-third of Chaudoc. More than 1,000 civilians were killed in Ben Tre and 2,000 in Hue, to cite only the better known of many examples. But what is more significant to the ultimate outcome of the war is that such barbarism is also accompanied by an ineffectuality—entirely aside from the question of politics and economics—which makes American failure in Vietnam inevitable.

Indiscriminate firepower is likely to hit civilian targets

simply because there are many more of them, and directly and indirectly that serves the purposes of the United States as all Administrations have defined them. But we know enough about mass firepower and strategic bombing to know that it is not only counterproductive politically, but also an immense waste militarily. As a land war, the Vietnam campaign for the U.S. has been a mixture of men and mobility via helicopters, with the N.L.F. generally free to fight at terms, places, and times of its own choosing. And because of ideology and allegiance, the N.L.F. always fills the critical organizational vacuum the Americans and their sponsored Saigon regime leave behind.

Even in the field, the American soldier lacks both motivation and a concept of the ideology and political nature of the war, which makes him tend toward terror and poor combat at one and the same time. Had he and his officers the will and knowledge to win—which, I must add, would scarcely suffice to attain victory—the American army would not be repeating the tale of My Lai over and over again. For My Lai is simply the foot soldier's direct expression of the axiom of fire and terror that his superiors in Washington devise and command from behind desks. No one should expect the infantryman to comprehend the truths about the self-defeating consequences of terror and repression that have escaped the generals and politicians. The real war criminals in history never fire guns, never suffer discomfort. The fact is, as the military discussions now reveal, that morale and motivation are low among troops, not merely toward the end of tours of duty or when combat follows no pattern and "morale goes down and down," to quote one Pentagon analyst, but also because an unwilling foreign conscript army has not and cannot in the twentieth century win a colonial intervention.

We can scarcely comprehend the war in Vietnam by concentrating on specific weapons and incidents, on My Lai, B-52s, or defoliants. What is illegal and immoral, a crime against the Vietnamese and against civilization as we think it should be, is the entire war and its intrinsic character. Mass bombing, the uprooting of populations, "search-and-destroy"—all this and far more are endemic to a war that can never be "legal" or moral so long as it is fought. For what is truly exceptional and unintended in Vietnam, from the Government's point of view, are the B-52 missions, defoliants, and artillery attacks that do not ravage villages and fields. Specific weapons and incidents are deplorable, but we must see them as effects and not causes. The major undesired, accidental aspect of the entire Vietnam experience, as three Administrations planned it, was that the Vietnamese resistance, with its unshakable roots everywhere in that tortured nation, would survive and ultimately prevail rather than be destroyed by the most intense rain of fire ever inflicted on men and women. For the history of America's role in Vietnam is not one of accident but rather of the failure of policy. Given what is so purposeful and necessary to the American war in Vietnam and the impossibility and undesirability of the United States relating to that nation by other than military means, there is only one way to terminate the endless war crimes systematically and daily committed there—to end the intrinsically criminal war now, to withdraw all American forces immediately. And while the Vietnamese succor and heal their wounds, Americans must attempt to cure their own moribund social illness so that this nation will never again commit such folly and profound evil.

JONATHAN SCHELL: One limitation in the reporting of Vietnam has been the tendency to concentrate on our actions and to ignore the effect of these actions on the Vietnamese. Even when we criticize the war, we tend to focus on *our* developments in technology, *our* changing weaponry.

Another kind of distortion results from the anecdotal nature of much reporting which creates the impression that Vietnam is a kind of playground for our idealism and cruelty.

There comes a point when one must realize that Vietnam has a limited number of villages and that the use of our evolving weaponry—the firepower that Professor Kolko has described—has been gradually smashing Vietnamese society, and the degree of this destruction is measurable.

In 1967, I spent a month in Quang Ngai province, where the My Lai massacre took place just a few months after I left. I flew in what they call forward air control planes—small Cessna single-propeller aircraft that are sent up to guide the bombers in their strikes. They do this with phosphorus rockets which not only mark the target but splash phosphorus over whatever they hit. They also attempt to find targets themselves in order to bring in other bombing planes.

When I first looked down from the plane over Quang Ngai province, I saw that the land below me had been completely devastated. It looked like a scene from World War II. I knew that the bombing in Vietnam had been of the enormity described by Professor Kolko, and I decided that I would attempt to survey Quang Ngai province from the air and on the ground to discover what the results of our bombing and our military presence had been, at least for this one province.

I flew for several weeks with military maps, shading the areas that were destroyed. Since the inhabited parts of Quang Ngai province are quite small—about forty miles long and five to ten miles wide—I was able to produce quite accurate statistics, which were later confirmed by checks on the ground and interviews with the three main ground commanders. What I discovered was that by the end of 1967, the destruction of society in Quang Ngai province was not something we were in danger of doing; it was a process we had almost completed. About 70 per cent of the villages in the province had been destroyed.

The destruction was brought about in a variety of ways. One of these ways was clearly described in some of the leaflets that were dropped by the millions over the province while I was there. The leaflets clearly spelled out a reprisal policy against villages suspected of helping the Vietcong. The comment has been made that the Vietnam war is waged not against the Vietcong but against the Vietnamese people. In that light, it is interesting to note that one leaflet is entitled "Marine Ultimatum to Vietnamese People" and its target is listed as "civilian population."

One side of the leaflet is illustrated with two drawings. The first shows several soldiers of the Vietcong setting up a mortar position near a thatched-roof house, while another soldier leans from a window firing an automatic weapon. A woman holding a child by the hand stands next to the house. Under the picture the caption reads, "If the Vietcong does this . . ." The second picture shows an Air Force jet pulling out of its dive over the house. An explosion in front of the house has thrown soldiers and the woman and child to the ground, and the house is in flames. In the foreground a man lies on the ground clutching his chest. Streams of blood flow from his eyes, nose, mouth, and ears. The rest of the pamphlet is in black and white, but this blood is printed in red ink. The second caption, completing the unfinished sentence of the first, reads, "Your village will look like this." In other words, "If the Vietcong does this, your village will look like this."

The other side of the leaflet reads:

Dear Citizens: The U.S. Marines are fighting alongside the Government of Vietnam forces in Duc Pho in order to give the Vietnamese people a chance to live a free, happy life without fear of hunger and suffering. But many Vietnamese have paid with their lives, and their homes have been destroyed, because they helped the Vietcong in an attempt to enslave the Vietnamese people. Many hamlets have been destroyed because these villages harbored the Vietcong. The hamlets of Hai Mon, Hai Tan, Sa Binh, Tan Binh, and many others have been destroyed because of this. We will not hesitate to destroy every hamlet that helps the Vietcong, who are powerless to stop the combined might of the Government of Vietnam and its allies. The U.S. Marines issue this warning: THE U.S. MARINES WILL NOT HESITATE TO DESTROY IMMEDIATELY ANY VILLAGE OR HAMLET HARBORING THE VIETCONG. WE WILL NOT HESITATE TO DESTROY IMMEDIATELY ANY VILLAGE OR HAMLET USED AS A VIETCONG STRONGHOLD TO FIRE AT OUR TROOPS OR AIRCRAFT. THE CHOICE IS YOURS. IF YOU REFUSE TO LET THE VIETCONG USE YOUR VILLAGES AND HAMLETS AS THEIR BATTLEFIELD, YOUR HOMES AND LIVES WILL BE SAVED. PEACEFUL CITIZENS, STAY IN YOUR HOMES, DENY YOUR SUPPORT TO THE VC'S.

Just in case the civilians didn't get the point from this leaflet clearly enough, in case they didn't get the point when the bombs actually fell on their village, another leaflet was dropped, whose title was "Your Village Has Been Bombed," and its target again was the civilian population. The second picture from the previous leaflet, showing the house aflame and the people dead, occupies a whole side of this leaflet. The caption reads, "The Vietcong caused this to happen." On the other side there is a ten-point text which includes these points: "(1) Your village was bombed becaused you harbored Vietcong in your village. (2) Your village was bombed because you gave help to the Vietcong in your area." Point number six, in case the villagers still haven't got the message is, "Your village will be bombed again if you harbor the Vietcong in any way."

Having ascertained the extent of the destruction in Quang Ngai province, I decided to fly over an operation from its beginning to its end in one of the forward air control planes. The operation was called BENTON and it was one of thirty or so proceeding against the Vietcong at that time—one of the many unreported operations that are continually under way. I brought my military maps with me again and charted out an area of several square kilometers which was said to have a population of 17,000. This was an area that had not yet been destroyed. I flew for two weeks with the forward air control planes, and what I saw day by day was the bombing of the villages and their burning by our ground troops.

If you go to the psychological warfare office at any major air base—such as Chu Lai, which I flew out of—you will be told the villages are not bombed unless they have been given warnings. At the end of this operation I went to the psychological warfare office at Chu Lai and asked for a full catalogue of the leaflets that had been dropped. I hardly needed to do this, because I had seen the people running from their burning homes, and I had seen no leaflets dropped prior to the bombings. Indeed, five or six leaflets had been dropped, and not one of them was a warning. They were such leaflets as this: "Appeal to the VC to reject the Red Chinese as their masters. The Red Chinese Communist masters of the Vietcong have declared that the South Vietnamese people must pay more and more to support the unjust war of the Vietcong," and so forth.

After I visited the psychological warfare office, I went to the civil affairs office and asked if there had been any evacuation of civilians during the operation. I learned that initially the colonel in charge of the operation had given an order that no refugees, as they call them, would be taken out of the area. Late in the operation that decision was reversed, and 100 of the 17,000 were taken out. But even those 100 were taken out after most of the area had been destroyed. In other words, an area inhabited by 17,000 people was about 70 per cent destroyed with no warning to the residents of the village, and with only 100 people evacuated from the area.

I would like to reflect briefly on the bearing this information has on the issue raised by several participants in this discussion: the relation of policy to reality.

It is certainly true that the orders handed to our soldiers when they arrive in Vietnam have little relation to the situation they actually face. Take, for example, the situation of a forward air control pilot who is sent up over an area of fields, jungle, and villages and who is instructed to guide bombers to targets and to find targets himself. There are no identifiable military structures at all, except perhaps for a few bunkers, and those are most likely to have been dug by civilians to protect themselves against our bombs. Yet the pilot must guide strikes; the bombers are coming in and he must find new targets.

Consequently, the realities of what happens in Vietnam are often the result of an incredible amount of improvisation by the people on the spot. The actual decisions about targets are made with an almost unbelievable casualness. The forward air control pilots, for example, who, of course, cannot tell the difference between an enemy soldier and a civilian from three thousand feet, find themselves attempting to make these distinctions. I asked one pilot how he could tell that a man whom he had identified as a Vietcong and had bombed was indeed a member of the Vietcong, and his answer was, "He has a bouncy gait; those shuffling farmers don't have a gait like that. He was a military man." This is not exceptional. I asked another pilot how he could tell the difference, and he said, "You get the hang of it. I can smell a Vietcong from five thousand feet." Still another said he could tell when trails had been used by the Vietcong because he could see bent grass.

If you have a target that is half a kilometer square—and that is often the closest pinpointing you get—how do you decide where to drop the bombs? Unbelievably childish criteria come into play. If it is an area with jungle and fields and huts, there is an impulse on the part of the pilots to bomb the huts, because they look like a target. Furthermore, the reports that have to be sent back to headquarters contain one blank for "military structures destroyed," so immediately after houses are bombed, the appropriate number of "military structures destroyed" is filled in on the chart. To convey the truth, the pilot would have to scrawl in, "Vietnamese houses bombed," and that would be most unlikely.

This is how the "reality," as perceived by the bureaucrats in the rear, is shaped to a large extent by the men at the front—right up there in the plane where the pilot is filling out his report. Much of the lawlessness in Vietnam occurs because the laws, or the orders handed down, have so little application to the situation the men actually face in the field.

Those who say that this vast destruction is a matter of policy are correct in a way, but I think it might be more accurate to say that the destruction is the inevitable result of a senseless policy that is actually impossible to carry out. Once this process is in motion, however, these senseless practices do tend to become legitimated, although they may never have been thought through by the bureaucrats in Washington or by the high military officers or by our political leaders.

Thus, the first time I witnessed the destruction of a village, the official line was that there had been no destruction of a village, that we never destroyed any villages. A year later, the line was that, well, it is true that we destroy villages and it is unfortunate, but it is necessary. A drift had taken place.

Our ultimate aim in going to Vietnam was not to achieve

military objectives or to have a high body count. Our objective was to create a government, democratic if it could be, that would stand after we left Vietnam. Yet the inevitable result of the level of destruction we have visited on Vietnam has been the dilution of the authority of the Saigon government. I saw election returns given out for villages in Quang Ngai province which I had seen lying deserted and in rubble the day before.

But we have utterly failed to establish a stable government in South Vietnam. It is too kind to call the Saigon government a dictatorship; it is more properly called a public relations job. It is not a government that is in danger of collapsing; it is a government that has collapsed over and over again—that has achieved only an unnatural existence wholly attributable to American support.

The fact that the government is as hopeless as it is leaves us with two basic alternatives in Vietnam. The first is simply to leave and to permit the Vietcong or the North Vietnamese or some combination of them to take over at their leisure. This may be regrettable, but I think it is what we have to face.

The second alternative is to continue what we are now doing—to commit more massacres and to destroy other provinces as we have destroyed Quang Ngai. This course of action—that is to say, our present course of action— leads to the total destruction of the society in South Vietnam. I don't think I need to tell you which of these courses I would advocate.

ARTHUR W. GALSTON: I would like to speak as a biologist, in this "Decade of the Environment," about one sense in which the Vietnam war is different from other wars. An entirely new tactic has arisen in Vietnam and has been designated "environmental warfare." I think the term is an apt one. It means the deliberate application of technology, mainly chemical, to so alter the ecology of a large region that permanent scars will be left.

Since 1962, our armed forces in Vietnam, working together with the South Vietnamese government and its armed forces, have sprayed about five million acres of land with more than one hundred million pounds of herbicidal chemicals. The object of this operation has been to defoliate trees affording cover for enemy forces and to kill certain plants, including rice, which furnish food for Vietcong forces and their civilian supporters. Most military observers consider that this has been a very successful military tactic which has spared many American lives.

Together with the use of about fourteen million pounds of CS gas, a so-called tear gas used to temporarily incapacitate combatants or to flush them out of hiding, this massive herbicidal spray operation constitutes a major resumption of chemical warfare operations, which had not been used much since the large-scale gas warfare of World War I. Many observers feel that our use of these agents violates both the Geneva Gas Protocol of 1925, which we wrote but never ratified, and the United Nations Resolution of 1966, to which we are signatory. The Geneva Gas Protocol bans the use in war "of asphyxiating, poisonous or other gases, and of all analogous liquids, materials or devices." This would certainly seem to include both herbicides and tear gases, but our one-time Ambassador to the United Nations, James Nabrit, specifically excluded these agents, which were normally used domestically, from inclusion under the Protocol.

Our military spokesmen have repeatedly stated that no permanent effects on the ecology of Vietnam can be expected to occur as a result of the massive use of herbicides, nor, they say, will there be any deleterious effects on man or his domestic animals. This is certainly an optimistic statement which many fear is not fully substantiated by the facts.

It is now quite clear that some long-range ecological defects have occurred. For one thing, the multiply defoliated timberlands are being invaded by bamboo, which normally cannot get a foothold in the dense shade of the understory vegetation. Once in a timberland, bamboo will be hard to get rid of, and since timber constitutes a major crop in South Vietnam, this could be a serious economic as well as ecological catastrophe. It has also been noted that the mangrove associations lining the estuaries of many of the Vietnamese rivers have been killed by single sprays with the phenoxyacetic acid herbicides, and that the time required for regeneration of this association, if, in fact, it ever comes back, would be about twenty to twenty-five years. The estuarine environment in which the mangroves grow is tremendously important to shellfish and migratory fish, which complete a portion of their life cycle in the ecosystem enveloped by the mangrove roots. With these plants killed, the fish will probably go elsewhere. This will lead to a decline in the fish and shellfish catch, which constitutes an important source of protein for the Vietnamese, whose diet is otherwise deficient in animal protein and essential amino acids.

Other ecological worries have to do with the possibility of increased soil erosion during the monsoonal rains as a consequence of the killing or weakening of vegetation stands. Also, since fully 50 per cent of the land of Vietnam is potentially lateralizable (i.e., the soil can be converted to a brick-like mass irreversibly if too much organic matter is removed), one has to face the possibility that we have permanently damaged some such agricultural land as well. We will not know whether or not these things have occurred until the war is over and there is an opportunity to conduct an adequate ecological survey in depth.

In the meantime, it appears that several of the herbicides previously considered innocuous to humans and animals can, in fact, be quite toxic. One of these, 2,4,5-tri-chlorophenoxyacetic acid (2,4,5-T) has been called teratogenic; that is, it is alleged to act like thalidomide in inducing abnormalities in developing embroyos in labora-tory mice and rats. By extrapolation, it is presumed to produce the same effects in other animals, including hu-mans. A calculation of the rate at which 2,4,5,-T is sprayed in Vietnam, plus some assumptions about rates of rainfall, indicate that Vietnamese women might have been con-suming teratogenic doses of 2,4,5-T. This, together with numerous recent newspaper reports of peculiar birth ab-normalities in Vietnam since late 1967, make one wonder whether, in fact, we have inadvertently caused medical catastrophes with presumably innocuous herbicidal chemicals. This matter requires further careful study and evaluation.

It seems clear that at best we will have produced a massive alteration of the vegetational complex of Viet-nam. At worst we may have produced permanent damage (mangroves might never recover, soil might be laterized) and we may have been responsible for inducing some abnormal births.

After the end of World War II, and as a result of the Nuremberg trials, we justly condemned the willful de-struction of an entire people and its culture, calling this crime against humanity *genocide*. It seems to me that the willful and permanent destruction of environment in which a people can live in a manner of their own choosing ought similarly to be considered as a crime against humanity, to be designated by the term *ecocide*. I believe that most highly developed nations have already commit-ted autoecocide over large parts of their own countries. At the present time, the United States stands alone as possi-bly having committed ecocide against another country, Vietnam, through its massive use of chemical defoliants and herbicides. The United Nations would appear to be an appropriate body for the formulation of a proposal against ecocide. If an international convention against ecocide is ever proposed, I would hope that the United States would be more prompt in ratifying it than it has been with the convention against genocide.

GEORGE WALD: Both the London Agreement and Charter and the Principles of Nuremberg include among Crimes Against Humanity "inhuman acts done against any civilian population." The Principles of Nuremberg declare explicitly that neither the internal law of states, nor an authoritative position in the state, nor—most important—the performance of such an act "pursuant to order of his Government or of a superior does not relieve him [i.e., one who performs such a crime] from responsibility under international law"—adding the curious qualification "provided a moral choice was in fact possible for him."

Ordinarily it seems to be taken for granted that what is stated here involves specifically *military* orders. The point I wish to raise is: If—as seems to be the case—under all the pressures of military discipline and even under combat conditions, a person or persons may be held criminally responsible for an unlawful act performed under the order of a superior, how much more should this be true of a presumably free agent, knowing fully the use to be made of his product, accepting a *business* order for it?

Take, for example, the German chemical manufacturers of the poison gas Zyklon, used in the extermination chambers. We treated the extermination chamber personnel as war criminals, regardless of the fact that they acted under the orders of superiors, civilian or military. Is not an industrial concern, which surely is free to make "a moral choice" and which is under no apparent discipline, for which therefore an "order" represents only an opportunity for profit—is not such an industrial concern considerably more culpable for its part in a "crime against humanity"?

I should like, from this point of view, to discuss the use of napalm against civilian objectives in Vietnam, and the responsibility incurred by its manufacturer, until recently the Dow Chemical Corporation. Dow began to produce napalm at its plant in Torrance, California, in 1966. Napalm is a jelly-like, inflammable mixture packed into canisters and dropped from planes on observed or suspected enemy targets. The materials are excessively simple: 25 per cent benzine, 25 per cent gasoline, and 50 per cent polystyrene, this last a plastic manufactured by Dow Chemical and others. The point of this mixture is to form a highly incendiary fluid that clings. It therefore causes deep and persistent burning.

It may be that the poison gas used in the gas chambers had civilian uses—for example, as a pesticide. That might then have been cited by its manufacturers as an extenuating circumstance. So far as I know, however, napalm has no other use than as a military weapon. Indeed, I think it has little use but as an anti-personnel weapon. Ordinarily, an explosive would be used for any operation intended to destroy physical facilities or installations.

Napalm is probably the most horrible anti-personnel weapon ever invented. The point of a weapon in war is to put an enemy out of action, and that is most readily and permanently accomplished by killing him; but civilized nations have tried not to induce more suffering than is necessary to accomplish this end. Napalm, in its means of action, in its capacity to maim permanently and to induce slow death, is a particularly horrifying weapon. That its use in Vietnam has involved many civilians—peasant families in undefended villages—has magnified the horror.

As a result, napalm early became a symbol to American students and others of their rejection of war, and specifically the Vietnam war. As early as 1966, pickets paraded at the Dow Chemical plant at Torrance and at the offices of the company in New York. In the years since, the appearance of a Dow representative to recruit personnel on a college or university campus frequently provoked a demonstration. Such demonstrations have occurred at Harvard, Princeton, the University of California, Wisconsin, Minnesota, and many other campuses.

After all this publicity and public rejection, one could hardly plead corporate unawareness on the part of Dow Chemical of what it was doing. If there is such a thing as individual or corporate responsibility for participating in a "crime against humanity," one could hardly find a better instance of it than this.

The principles stated in the London Agreement and Charter and in the Principles of Nuremberg were given effect by the Control Council for Germany, composed of the military commanders of the four occupied zones of Germany, in Control Council Law No. 10. Under Law No. 10, the United States conducted twelve trials at Nuremberg before American tribunals. Article II recognized among war crimes "atrocities or offenses against persons or property constituting violations of the laws or customs of war, including, but not limited to, murder, ill-treatment or deportation to slave labor or for any other purpose, of civilian populations, . . . murder or ill-treatment of prisoners-of-war, . . . killing of hostages, . . . wanton destruction of cities, towns or villages or devastation not justified by military necessity."

Among Crimes Against Humanity it included "atrocities and offenses, including but not limited to murder, extermination, enslavement, deportation, imprisonment, torture, rape or other inhuman acts committed against any civilian population. . . ." Article II went on to declare that "any person, without regard to nationality or the capacity in which he acted, is deemed to have committed" such crimes "if he was (a) a principal, or (b) an accessory to the commission of any such crime or ordered or abetted the same, or (c) took a consenting part therein, or (d) was connected with plans or enterprises involving its commission, or (e) was a member of any organization or group connected with the commission of any such crime."

Law No. 10 also restated the principle of personal responsibility: "The fact that any person acted pursuant to the order of his government or of a superior does not free him from responsibility for a crime but may be considered in mitigation."

If—as seems to me possible—some of the reported uses of napalm in Vietnam fit the definitions of war crimes and crimes against humanity, particularly as this weapon affected civilian populations, it would seem that a case might be made for holding the manufacturer of this weapon responsible as "an accessory" or as a consenting partner, or surely as an agency "connected with plans or enterprises involving its commission" or as "a member of an organization or group connected with the commission of any such crime."

What particularly singles out such a weapon as napalm in this connection? I think it is a principle of indiscriminateness of action, of failure to select its victims. Members of our armed forces are facing court-martial for having killed civilians who were clearly visible and hence identifiable as such. In prosecuting such cases we recognize officially that it is a war crime or crime against humanity to select the wrong persons (e.g., unarmed civilians) to kill. It seems to me to be only an extension of the same principle to regard as criminal nonselective killing, i.e., killing without selecting the right persons (i.e., military personnel) to kill. This is the principle that lies behind the attempt in war to attack only military objectives. The blind destruction of whole villages with artillery or from the air, on the grounds that one had drawn fire from somewhere in these villages, would seem on this basis to constitute a war crime. The very nature of napalm invites such nonse-lective killing, invites uses that can hardly be confined to military objectives. In part that is what makes it such a reprehensible weapon in its very nature.

If this last argument seems somewhat tenuous, it is curi-ous to realize that the special reprehensibility of such weapons is well understood by all concerned. There are weapons that governments and armed forces are proud of and put on public display. There are other weapons that are hidden, that are talked about as little as possible—not for security reasons, since they need not involve military secrecy in the usual sense, but because their use and mode of action might arouse public dismay, horror, and perhaps active opposition. Napalm, the nerve gases, indeed all poison gases, herbicides and defoliants, and all the weap-ons of biological warfare—pathogenic bacteria, viruses, and toxins—all are of this nature. Everyone concerned in ordering, producing, or using them tries in every way possible to avoid publicity.

It is interesting to realize that this was true long before the Principles of Nuremberg were enunciated. One had already such well-recognized codes of "laws of war" as contained in the Hague Convention of 1907.

In any case, when the great German chemical trust, I. G. Farben, began in 1939 to develop a war gas program, it went to considerable lengths to conceal the operation, as a matter of corporate—not military—secrecy. I. G. Farben organized a 100 per cent subsidiary, Luranil, for the construction of plants, and another one, Anorgana, for their operation. These were cover names to conceal own-ership and partly to relieve I. G. Farben of responsibility, but the capital was owned by I. G. Farben.

Dow Chemical manufactured napalm quite openly. Yet its responses to criticism on this score reveal a strange degree of defensiveness and consciousness of vulnerabil-ity. Take, for example, the statement of Herbert D. Doan, the president of Dow Chemical, in *The Wall Street Journal* in December, 1967:

> Why do we produce napalm? In simplest form, we produce it because we feel our company should produce those items which our fighting men need in time of war when we have the ability to do so.
>
> A quarter of a century ago this answer would have satisfied just about everyone who asked this question. Today, however, it doesn't. Today we find ourselves accused of being immoral because we produce this product for use in what some people consider unjust war. We are told that to make a weapon because you're asked to do so by your Government puts you in precisely the same position as the German industrialists who pleaded at their Nuremberg trials that they were "only following orders."
>
> What of the argument that we are no different from the German industrialists who "just followed orders"? We reject the validity of comparing our present form of government with Hitler's Nazi Germany. In our mind our Government is still representative of and responsive to the will of the people.
>
> Our critics ask if we are willing to stand judgment for our choice to support our Government if history should prove this wrong. Our answer is yes. . . .

Actually, despite this last declaration by its president, Dow Chemical had issued earlier a formal statement disavowing exactly the kind of responsibility that our Government agrees exists under the Principles of Nuremberg:

> Our position on the manufacture of napalm is that we are a supplier of goods to the Defense Department and not a policymaker. We do not and should not try to decide military strategy or policy. Simple good citizenship requires that we supply our Government and our military with those

goods which they feel they need whenever we have the technology and capability and have been chosen by the Government as a supplier.

We will do our best, as we always have, to try to produce what our Defense Department and our soldiers need in any war situation. Purely aside from our duty to do this, we will feel deeply gratified if what we are able to provide helps to protect our fighting men or to speed the day when the fighting will end.*

It is curious to expect fighting men under all the stresses of combat to exercise a degree of personal responsibility and judgment that a large civilian corporation so lightly disclaims.

Dow made a further argument that seemed to it important, and was widely used by its representatives on campuses, though its relevance seems somewhat questionable:

In terms of dollars, the contract was a small one in the range of $5 million in 1966, or about one-fourth of one per cent of the company's total sales. The profit involved was of little material significance.

There was even a letter from former Secretary of Defense Robert S. McNamara to Herbert D. Doan, written in 1967:

There are also charges that your company is a war profiteer, charges made by persons ignorant of the purchasing procedures of the Department of Defense and of your company's role as a defense supplier. As you will know, our contracting procedures ensure that there can be no profiteering. . . .

This position leaves something to explain. In playing down the napalm operation, Dow stated that the plant at

*Don Whitehead, *The Dow Story,* McGraw-Hill Book Co., Inc. New York: 1968, p. 264.

Torrance "employed less than a dozen workers." Since the materials of napalm are the simplest and cheapest, it is a little difficult to understand why the contract should have come to $5 million in 1966, and apparently had increased to $10 million in 1969, when Dow permitted itself to be outbid on the napalm contract by American Electric Company of Los Angeles. One might well ask what considerations prompted Dow to drop out of this contract; since, as it said, the profit was of little significance, one might have hoped that its sense of "simple good citizenship" might have prompted Dow to keep the contract going.

The tribunals that conducted the Nuremberg trials were cognizant throughout that they were acting within a restricted situation, creating certain precedents in accordance with it, but that actions and precedents established later would expand and deepen the applicability of the Principles. One limitation in their original application, for example, was that they were alleged by the defense to be retroactive, since the Principles of Nuremberg had not been stated when the offenses occurred. Now that we have lived with the Principles of Nuremberg for twenty years, their applicability can no longer be questioned on this ground, and there is every reason to explore and develop their implications further.

It is of some interest that an attempt is now being made to bring a civil action against the Dow Chemical Corporation in the United States District Court for the District of Columbia, to try to compel the corporation to stop producing chemical and biological weapons thought to be in violation of international law. The chief counsel in presenting this complaint is Professor Alan W. Scheflin of the Georgetown University Law Center. The suit refers to Dow's production and sale of "various types of chemical, biological, bacteriological, incendiary and asphyxiatory weapons." There is a list of more than sixty-five plaintiffs, including professors in various fields, scientists, clergy-men in all the major denominations, and members and officials of a wide variety of civil organizations. This suit was filed on February 3, 1970, and is awaiting disposal.

MICHAEL MACCOBY: I would like to raise the question of the relevance of the United Nations Genocide Convention in 1948 (which the United States has not yet ratified) to our discussion of developments in Vietnam. Jean-Paul Sartre has suggested that the concept of genocide is applicable to wars waged by a highly technological society, such as ours, against an underdeveloped society, such as that of Vietnam.

When the high technology of modern warfare is brought to bear against a population such as the Viet-namese—or the Algerian peasants or a series of other peasant societies that have fallen victim to more advanced industrial nations since the end of the nineteenth century —is it not inevitable that the result will be genocide? If the Senate were to hold hearings on ratification of the Genocide Convention, as President Nixon has urged, would this not have a bearing on the conduct of the Viet-nam war and on the general conduct of American policy?

TELFORD TAYLOR: The idea of genocide—the concept, the word—was developed simultaneously with the Nuremberg trials. It arose out of the plain demonstration that Nazi policy was specifically directed against certain racial groups, primarily the Jews.

For lawyers the concept of genocide has always been a bit ambiguous, since it simply condemns doing on a large scale for a specific objective of a racial nature what it is already criminal to do on a small scale.

It seems to me that our initial failure to ratify the Geno-cide Convention was a grave political mistake. The rea-sons for it are now a matter of rather ancient history, but

I feel it would still be a wise thing to do. I am concerned, however, that at this time—because of the problems that have arisen in Vietnam—action in ratifying the Genocide Convention may seem to be an easy way to make a show of humanitarianism and respect for the law without really probing our own conduct.

RICHARD FALK: One problem posed by the Genocide Convention and its submission to the Senate for ratification at this point is that to do so would sharpen the contradiction between creed and conduct. At the very time when the United States Government is conducting a war that many of us affirm is genocidal, can that same Government in good conscience submit to its own legislative bodies a convention on genocide?

There is much talk of "no more Vietnams," but our policies in the Third World are based on the support of governments that can only survive if we are prepared to engage in more Vietnams. Many of these governments are suppressing their own populations. They are isolated governments, confronted by populations that can easily be aroused to support revolutionary movements. The only way to prevent those revolutionary movements from succeeding is to be prepared to engage in more Vietnams. And we have no military capability or political capability that allows us to wage Vietnams without committing war crimes on a massive scale that tends toward genocide.

It seems very important to expose this basic contradiction in as clear a manner as possible. If Senate hearings on the Genocide Convention were to provide such an educational opportunity, they would potentially be a very valuable forum. But if this is just another My Lai prosecution—another attempt to isolate the wrongdoing and dissociate ourselves from it—then I think its effect could be most detrimental.

DANIEL ELLSBERG: I have misgivings about the use of the word "genocide" in the context of the Vietnam war as it has been conducted up to this point. It may, indeed, be applicable, in a strict sense, to some of our activities in Vietnam, in particular the designation of large, semi-permanent, free-fire zones. Other activities, such as the massive generation of refugees, both deliberate and inadvertent, might warrant the term "sociocide," the violent destruction of a patterned society; still others, the term "ecocide" that has just been introduced.

Nevertheless, an indiscriminate use of such terms can blur potentially important distinctions about levels of destructiveness. An escalation of rhetoric can blind us to the fact that Vietnam is not only no more brutal than other wars in the past—and it is absurdly unhistorical to insist that it is—but that the Vietnam war is not as bad as other wars that we may have in the near future. And it is not as bad as it could still become. We must remain able to recognize the possibility of the occurrence of such increases in violence and risk, if we are to act to deter them or reverse them.

Thus, I suspect that because critics of the war in 1966 and 1967 tended to exaggerate the effect of the war on the population of Vietnam—as bad as it was then—they failed to discover that in 1968, even after the Tet and May crises, the war became enormously more destructive than it had ever been before. This increase, described to me by participating officials, was a result of changes in our policies that went almost totally unnoticed.

At the time of Tet, with the Vietcong entering the cities for the first time, we dropped the restraints we had previously imposed on the use of helicopter gunships and artillery in populated areas. For a period of several months, almost all of Vietnam became a free-fire zone. Subsequently, the designation of free-fire zones became much more widespread than it had been before. A new generation of helicopter pilots and artillery men came into rural

Vietnam beginning in the late spring of 1968, found these new practices that had been instituted because of the back-to-the-wall conditions that surrounded the Tet offensive, and regarded them as normal.

Though the verbal orders have changed somewhat since then, the practices, I am told, have not. Since 1968, the citizens of Vietnam have been under fire in a way that did not apply in 1966 and 1967, although given their flight to the towns and the reduced level of combat, actual casualties are probably less than in 1968. Interrogations of Vietcong prisoners reveal that their greatest miscalculation in launching the Tet offensive was their failure to anticipate the enormous casualties they would sustain. It simply did not occur to them that the United States would be willing to launch firepower as freely as it did in populated areas. The Vietcong felt they would be shielded and protected by the population, but they were not.

In March, 1968, we also came perilously close to a decision that would probably have led to the invasion of North Vietnam. This would have been the likely indirect and ultimate consequence if we had granted the troop increase requested by General William C. Westmoreland. We would then have entered upon a war incomparably more destructive than anything we have witnessed so far in Vietnam.

The population of South Vietnam has almost surely increased each year in the last five, and the use of the word "genocide" can, therefore, be misleading, even if it is strictly warranted. But if we had invaded North Vietnam and totally unleashed our bombing, the population of neither North Vietnam nor South Vietnam would have increased. In that case, the word "genocide" in its most ominous sense would have come closer to reality.

Finally, if nuclear weapons had been used, as I have been told was contemplated at high levels in connection with the defense of Khe Sanh, a degree of destructiveness incomparably surpassing anything we have yet seen in Vietnam would have come into play.

Without compromising our protest against the Vietnam war as it has actually evolved, we need to maintain reserves of outrage and resistance, and words and perceptions to trigger them, if we are to prevent tragedies still worse.

I see difficulties, too, in the distinctions we draw between the use of high and low technology. My Lai, after all, was not a question of unrestrained use of advanced technology. It was a use of World War I—if not Civil War —weaponry against people. The use of guns, rifles, small arms, stray bullets, the use of grenades, face-to-face killing —that certainly does not rely upon very advanced technology.

There is a tendency to confine the applicability of the war crimes concept just to such crimes of low technology. The concept, after all, dates from a period of low technology, around the time of World War I, and weaponry that has come into use since then has tended to be excluded.

This emphasis on low-technology war crimes tends to absolve our use of high-technology weapons—such as B-52s, carrier aircraft, helicopter gunships, CBW bombs —which are our main implements of death, in the Vietnam war specifically. These products are, in fact, regarded very highly by our culture—Western culture in general but, above all, American culture. To condemn the unrestrained use of complex, highly developed technologies is to defy some of our proudest national values. It will be difficult, politically, to extend the notion of "crimes against humanity" to include Anglo-American wartime triumphs of firepower against civilians, as in Dresden, Tokyo, Hiroshima, and now the free-fire zones of South Vietnam. Yet it would be shocking and perverse to condemn only rape and murder in wartime while continuing to tolerate the strategic bombing of noncombatants.

Furthermore, to define atrocities in terms of perpetrators who "looked upon the faces of their victims"—another aspect of current usage—is to say that only those who can see the faces of their victims are, in fact, war criminals. One aspect of such a definition—not, I suspect, a coincidental one—is that it excludes almost everyone above the rank of captain. Only the lowest-ranking soldiers in a war, and not too many of them, ever see the faces of their victims. To depart from that rule—to hold accountable, for instance, the majors who fly in airplanes, let alone the people who command them or who plan their missions—is to lead, of course, to the highest ranks of the military and above that to the highest civilians in the Government. But that, too, is a direction in which we must go.

MARCUS RASKIN: I would use the term "high technology" in a very broad sense, applying it not only to weapons but also to the organization of the use of weapons. We may be concerned with a man shooting a rifle, but to get that man into combat required the most sophisticated weaponry, the most sophisticated organizational structure, the most sophisticated system of planning. In the field, the Vietnam war may not appear to involve much high technology, but if you look at the organizing for war in a country like United States you find a very high technological organizational skill devoted to this activity, whether it be a limited war or a nuclear war.

Indeed, the entire system of attempting to "modernize" other nations through the use of military means should be called into question, as should the use of nuclear weapons to "defend" other nations against attack. The introduction of nuclear weapons may itself be intolerable, since it will be too late to make a judgment about those weapons once they are used.

That is why it is absolutely crucial to make judgments about the whole structure of technology. If it is given over to such purposes, it must turn out to be totalitarian. It must result in a perpetuation of these wars—not only in Vietnam, but in Laos, in Bolivia, and ultimately in the United States—for those tactics and strategies that are employed at the edges of an empire eventually end up being used at home. We already see them beginning to be applied within the United States.

GABRIEL KOLKO: I would emphasize one aspect of Mr. Schell's presentation: The very process by which the Pentagon comes to the Congressional committees on appropriations and requests funds for 130,000 tons of bombs a month assumes certain acts and certain human consequences. While it is possible for some variations to occur in Vietnam because of decisions made by commanders there, the fact remains that those commanders have the obligation and duty to drop 130,000 tons a month, and the only way they can do it, given the limited number of military targets, is to drop those bombs indiscriminately on whatever moves.

No one should be under the illusion that what is going on in Vietnam is not in principle and in essence calculated, planned, and intended. I think it is very much a part of a deliberate objective—one that is certainly understood by the people in the Pentagon. They certainly understand that villages are being targeted and hit every day in immense quantities and that those 130,000 tons of bombs are being dropped on the peasants.

WILLIAM R. CORSON: Consideration of the full implications of American activities in Vietnam is long overdue, not only because the effects of its schizophrenia-inducing pressures on those who fought the war must be understood if future Vietnams and similar catastrophes are to be avoided, but also because the Vietnam war fully and completely reveals the incompatibility between our policy and politics. Seen in this light, the abhorrent revelations concerning My Lai, the use of napalm, etc., begin to acquire some perspective. The legality or illegality of these acts is not really the question we need to address. The question, more properly, is did these acts occur as aberrations or did they occur as a result of the incompatibility between our policy and our politics? I suggest they occurred because of the incompatibility. Since 1947 we have not fully perceived the changing nature of war. Those who have been charged with determination of policy have acted like generals: Their policy has been designed to address the last war and not the one we find ourselves confronted with today.

Since 1947 the incompatibility between our policy and politics has been well illustrated by the degree of American participation in the five major guerrilla conflicts against Asian non-Communist, Western allied, or Western colonial regimes. In the unsuccessful guerrilla conflicts in the Philippines and Malaya, United States participation or assistance was minimal. However, from the Communist conquest of China through the Vietminh struggle against the colonial French-Indochina regime and finally to the yet undecided Vietcong war, the politics of our policy has escalated from limited assistance to the *status quo* power into a massive direct involvement of American prestige and might. Our politics of an ever-increasing escalatory response has pushed us perilously close to taking on a larger enemy than our policy requires. Administration spokesmen, both of the Nixon regime and of those which preceded it, have been reduced to saying that we insist our long-suffering South Vietnamese allies get to heaven or hell without interference from the North, and that we will defend to the death their inherent right to seek oblivion or exaltation in their own way.

I am not willing to reject outright the claim of those who say we are engaged in a historic test for halting covert violence across *de facto* frontiers. They have elaborated the notion that over the last twenty years the Communist experiment in guerrilla warfare has fallen apart at one point after another—in Indochina, Burma, Malaya, Indonesia, the Philippines, and Korea—until Mao Tsetung's doctrine is now finally exposed and at stake in Vietnam. Convinced that we are confronting Mao's last stand, they take succor from General Vo Nguyen Giap, himself, who reportedly says, "South Vietnam is the model of the National Liberation movement in our time."

They also claim the Vietnam outcome will be the decisive test for the allegedly historic Sino-Soviet dispute over wars of national liberation and how far to press them. I say allegedly because the Sino-Soviet argument over relative degrees of adventurism in crossing frontiers with arms and men has not been borne out in Vietnam, where despite their loud voices the Chinese have so far been markedly circumspect about their own degree of intervention. But in spite of these conditions, many are saying that Vietnam will have a decisive impact on everybody's calculations, that the idea of applying incremental violence across frontiers will be choked off in a manner that will stifle recurrence, and that the agonies for us in responding sensationally to nonsensational aggression will perhaps abate once we have successfully passed this particular watershed. Yet I have much greater faith in the future of force in politics than is allowed by this neo-Wilsonian notion of a war to end all wars of liberation. Because of this belief in the persistence of force as part of the political process, I am both alarmed and, at the same time, encouraged by the interest and emphasis placed on understanding the real meaning of America's combat involvement in Vietnam.

However, Vietnam continues to smash the models and spoil the theories. Because our current doctrine does not allow for politically motivated decisions and because conditions no longer conform, our doctrine has been shaken by the facts. This is not the first time military/political doctrine has been overtaken by events, nor will it be the last, but rather than adapting to a changed situation, we persevere. We are told that success in Vietnam will mean final deterrence for externally supported aggression, but our common sense makes us doubt it.

As we and our adversaries look at the current level of hostilities and the risks and strains of our current involvement, these factors, far from assuring future deterrence, lead to speculation that even if in some net sense we succeed, we still might not do it again. Our behavior during the Arab-Israeli Six Day War in 1967 was immediately read in many capitals as a disinclination to repeat involvement. Whatever the conventional wisdom says, doubts and ambiguities systematically left open do not necessarily translate into deterrents. Yet we have been driving our doctrine on and on beyond Vietnam, beyond our effort there to freeze the use of force across frontiers. We have gone on to embrace the foreclosing of force at level after level within frontiers as well.

It has become fashionable to think and say that force used against established order anywhere in the nuclear world is potentially escalatory to world-crisis dimensions. If so, it is arguably in our national interests to diminish protesting force as much as possible and to bolster established authority wherever it is not currently opposed to us.

Now if, indeed, we cannot really expect Vietnam to be the external war to end all internal wars, how much more problematical must our expectations be when we move from what we are pleased to call "external war" and "internal war" to attempt the freezing of force at even lower levels in the elusive environments of preinsurgency and incipient unrest. One need not accept unequivocally the Maoist doctrine that political power grows out of the barrel of a gun to understand that internal violence is normal for most countries and that those who would restrain, reduce, remove, or concentrate this violence have a special obligation to think clearly about means and ends.

Nobody wants to be naïve any more about the unavoidability, necessity, and legitimacy of force—provided the time and place are right. A body of literature has developed dealing with protracted conflict, game theories of force, and appropriate levels of violence. Within the Federal Government, ever-expanding bands of harassed bureaucrats speak casually about strategies of conflict and cling lightheartedly to concepts of deterrence before, while, and after deterrence fails. This exposure to conceptions of limited war, insurgency, or whatever you may choose to call it is not bad *per se*, but we tend to underrate the many different guises and auspices under which guerrilla warfare may appear.

Acceptance without question or modification of the rich complexity of guerrilla war experience separates those who desire to make policy from those who wish to examine policy before it is adopted. No one who is anxious for a hearing in the policy councils allows himself to think that the suppression of violence by violence is *a priori* inadmissible. The issue is how to discriminate constructively in the use and non-use of violence. Superficially, it is easy to accept the premise of *quid pro quo* violence. The biblical injunction of an eye for an eye lends moral credence to its acceptance. However, the actual results of translating the premise into a practical course of action are alarming.

We have seen in Vietnam the difficulties posed by the nature of a guerrilla war, where there are no fixed lines, where the enemy usually does not wear uniforms, and where he employs terror as a routine instrument of warfare. In such a war there are many gray areas. There are no agreed-to rules of land warfare which stipulate the rules when one of the antagonists is a regular force of either the attacked government or an outside government and the other includes old men, women, and children, as well as guerrilla troops. And it is doubtful such rules can ever be written. Lacking such rules, if the United States is to avoid the moral and legal dilemmas associated with brutality in warfare, not only the American fighting man but the entire American society must have a thorough knowledge of the national end in view and of the methods used by other democratic nations under similar conditions. Such knowledge has been consistently absent throughout the Vietnam war. Regardless of the outcome of the My Lai courts-martial and other legal actions, the point remains that American judgment of the effective prosecution of the war was faulty from beginning to end and that the atrocities, alleged or otherwise, are a result of a failure of judgment, not criminal behavior. There is scant comfort in such a statement for those who consider themselves to be "doves" on the matter of the Vietnam war, but this is the case.

As a nation we abdicated our responsibility to differentiate between means and ends in the execution of our foreign policy. We turned this responsibility over to an Executive who is not bound in the conduct of foreign policy by much more than his own perception of the world and the consciences of those who surround and advise him. The results of this abdication should be abundantly clear to the nation today, and we do not serve the long-term interests of the United States, by pointing a finger of accusation at those who carried out that policy as best they understood it in ways which are now, after the fact, morally repugnant and perhaps legally indefensible. The conduct of the general, the colonel, the lieutenant, or the sergeant who believes that the way to stop aggression in Vietnam is to eliminate all who may be potential aggressors is not inconsistent with his training and background. The military forces of the United States will do as they are told to do. However, the absence of the kind of direction which says it is erroneous, illegal, and immoral to kill people without clear military advantage in a war shifts the responsibility for the judgment of how best to achieve a political end through military force to persons who, by their nature, training, and background, are ill-equipped to make such a judgment.

We delude ourselves with the belief that the stress on our self-image will be removed by any legal or quasi-legal proceedings. We never established what we wanted in Vietnam, and it became possible, therefore, to justify or rationalize any military action in terms of some dubious military advantage. We should not be surprised at the chaos such ambiguity has produced. Hitler at least identified the target for his soldiers, whereas our soldiers have been forced into the position where the distinction between friend and foe has been blurred beyond recognition by national policy statements and such anomalies as free-fire zones. This confusion in no way excuses, sanctions, or condones wanton murder, but it helps explain how the beast which lurks in us all has been unleashed because our forces in Vietnam did not know what they are doing and why.

How useful is our attempt to place Vietnam in a moral context? Does it help or hinder us in making discriminating judgments, in distinguishing symptoms from causes and irrelevancies from relevancies? How much does it condition us to distort our own national impact on other people's politics? How can we avoid the increasing paradox that the means we have used in Vietnam, as a kind of international lethal aid society, leave us psychologically unprepared to undertake the most sensitive kind of intervention at the same time that our budgets, motivations, and civilian incentives for more popular politics abroad decline? In such a context it is no accident we became overinvolved militarily and underinvolved politically in the human forces of the future.

This paradox carries fateful consequences, for it increases the tension between America's domestic political value system and a contrasting international political value system. Only a more controlled and deliberate approach can reduce this tension—only more intelligently determined choices of where and how to intervene and where and how not to. To what insurgencies or insurrectional situations should we respond? How do we keep short-term perspectives from driving out longer-term perspectives? How do we apply self-denying ordinances more effectively? When we must try to counter the next insurgency by arming the incumbent one, how can we remove the stigma from our intervention? How can we identify constructively with the moving forces of history while separating ourselves from the forces that are historically on the way out? How can the opposition, as well as the government, be associated with our efforts? How can our presence be kept from contributing to the feebleness and timidity of civil institutions and weighting the local scales once more in favor of already prevalent military politics? How can we keep from enacting legitimacy illegitimately—in situations where notions of legitimacy are artificial and self-serving and where the psychological acceptance of legitimacy as a concept is often totally lacking among the human instruments through which our forces and officials must operate? How do we assure that our efforts will keep to their appropriately marginal role as a justifiable adjunct of the constructive but disruptive process of modernization? How can we stop the host military from switching from house painting back to house arrests, giving up well digging for execution, moving from civil action to civil suppression, using the implements we have provided against the people in whose name and for whose protection the equipment has been given? How can our politics and policy be made to protect us, and a people we are trying to help, from actions of the military in their nation?

The lack of answers to these questions reveals, in spite of the changed military technology, how little war has changed over the centuries. Yet these same questions underscore the potential for making war less a tragedy for our nation than it has become as a result of our entering Vietnam without considering the questions, let alone determining their answers.

Even if we grant, for the sake of argument, the currently fashionable theory that the world's military will surprise us one day by turning the so-called national armies into real national armies and will become the acknowledged wombs of equality, the agents of incorruptibility, the bearers of land reform, the custodians of disinterested good will, and the conveyors of popular democracy—even so, not many of them have surprised us yet. We still need to weigh the consequences of overinvesting in the military process. Within the context of Vietnam, this is not only a question of the physical presence of the U.S. Army or Marine Corps, a Special Forces A Team or a MAAG, or advisers, technicians, and researchers. Nor is it merely a question of whether the food cartons outnumber the ammunition boxes, both bearing the clasped-hand symbol "gift of the American people." Instead it is really a question of the total posture struck, pronouncements made, deals consummated, constructive opportunities missed, friendships and enmities acquired—in short, the overall impact of the vast range of active and passive Americans simultaneously involved with or involved in country "X."

Obviously there is a personal hedge in my remarks, based on my belief that these questions are not likely to be addressed, that we will carry on our present practices in other areas of the world on the forlorn hope that perhaps the Lord looks after the United States, children, and drunks. Personally, this expectation of religious intervention on the side of the United States does not encourage me. We have made many errors in Vietnam, and there seems to be little intention on the part of those currently in charge to understand the nature of those errors and to mend our ways. Failure to do this can only ensure that the nature of war in the future will be more brutal, more indiscriminate, and more counterproductive. Perhaps, as we try to understand what our combat involvement in Vietnam has really meant to this nation, it would be well to listen to the attitude of one military man who was asked about the meaning of the Nuremberg trials. His comment is disturbing, not merely because of the intellectual bereftness it reflects, but more importantly because of the realism of the professional soldier in his belief that the citizens he serves are unwilling to provide him with the guidance to accomplish the genuine goals of the nation. His statement about the trials and their meaning to him and his future was simply, "Nuremberg proves one thing: You better win."

MARCUS RASKIN: The Vietnam war must be understood as part of a general process that has been going on over the last several decades—a process based on four principal components: a large bureaucracy, an armed force, a high technology, and a doctrine—the doctrine of limited war. All of these have come together in a hunt for threat situations. In 1961, for example, Secretary of Defense Robert S. McNamara asked a lieutenant general on his staff to prepare a list of the "threats" to the world. He came up with sixteen situations, and then each of the armed services undertook to show how it would respond to the sixteen "threats."

This sort of procedure raises some basic questions: Who defines such terms as "threat" and "enemy"? Who decides which situations require intervention by force—including the force of nuclear arms? We must lay out a very different framework of judgment and doctrine—one that insists that certain things are indeed not permissible.

MICHAEL MACCOBY: At the heart of much of our discussion lies a process of moral and psychological change that has been going on in this century. We have seen the triumph of the values of industrial bureaucracy—efficiency, measuring of results by numbers, productivity for its own sake, predictability—over such values as compassion and cultural richness, which tend to get in the way of efficiency.

I would note that this is not just due to capitalism, as some people would think. The same process has occurred in the Soviet Union; Stalin's attitude towards the peasants after the Russian Revolution was that all those who would not conform to the state's plan of industrial bureaucracy had to be systematically destroyed.

There is a similar example in the history of the Mexican Revolution. The government, in fighting against Zapata, built up villages for friendly peasants, called it a "pacification program," and shot any Mexican peasant outside who wore—in that instance—"white pajamas." The result was to completely radicalize the population and change the nature of the conflict from a small, conservative peasant rebellion to a total war against the entire population. In waging such a war, according to principles of industrial bureaucracy and efficiency, one must attack the sources of supply, which in the case of peasant populations are not factories but families, homes, and fields.

This historic trend does not prove that man is evil by nature or that wars must always be like that. It does demonstrate that the changing values to which I referred have a logic of their own and force people into a course of conduct in which compassion becomes a sin rather than a virtue. Unless one looks at this historic process and its psychological and moral effects, it is impossible to comprehend the enormity of our actions. If we do not confront this historic task, perhaps civilization will never have a chance to confront it again.

RICHARD BARNET: One of the problems in assessing responsibility in the upper reaches of government is the phenomenon of denial that you find throughout the entire bureaucratic apparatus.

Our Government has insisted, for example, that the bombing raids conducted against North Vietnam were never aimed at the destruction of purely civilian targets. I was in North Vietnam in November, 1969, and visited one village where I was told that 20,000 people had lived. From the size of the area and similar villages, I would regard that as a credible estimate. But all that was left of that village when I was there were seven fragments of wall. I went to another town, where I was told there had been 40,000 people, and this one, too, was totally wiped out. During a day-and-a-half visit to Thanh Hoa province, I saw more than ten Roman Catholic churches and about an equal number of pagodas that had been destroyed.

When I returned and told a very high official of the last Administration that I was sure there must have been either a policy of totally indiscriminate bombing or a deliberate policy of bombing such population centers, he assured me that I was mistaken. "As a matter of fact," he said, "I know just what you're talking about. All of those churches are places where the North Vietnamese hide their trucks." Well, most of the churches I saw were literally in the middle of rice fields and could not have been used to hide a truck or anything else; there would be no way to get a truck from the road to these buildings.

I think that the man I talked to really did believe what he had been told. And what happens, I suspect, is that the reality gets filtered out all up the line, so that the people at the top really believe that indiscriminate bombing does not, in fact, take place. What this suggests is that the vague limits that may be imposed by policy at the top are impossible to police or enforce. I doubt that the Vietnam war— or any counterinsurgency war—can be fought without committing war crimes within the definition established by past precedent.

Can any country such as the United States, with its predominant military and economic power, with a position so commanding in the world, carry out warfare against a weaker state, without in fact pressing its advantage to the limit of its own assessment of its own security? When the United States has exercised restraint, it has done so only in response to perceived threats from a stronger or equally strong power.

The basic issues is the permissibility of basing a foreign policy on our unilateral determination to use violence whenever and wherever we see fit, to achieve ends as we determine them. This basic notion of how we use our military power really has to be attacked before we can work out ground rules for managing the violence on the battlefields.

PHILIP NOEL-BAKER: I believe that it is true that bombings and atrocities do nothing but strengthen the national feeling for resistance. I happen, by a chance of family history, to have a home in Greece. Every time I drive home from the Athens airport to my country retreat, I pass a metal plaque set in a rock by the roadside which records that the Germans shot seventy-six innocent Greek civilians in reprisal for some act of sabotage. It was such acts of terror that steeled the Greeks in their heroic resistance against the joint invasion of the Nazis and Facists in World War II—a resistance that played a great part in the ultimate victory of the Allies.

I recall, too, the story of Winston Churchill, who went down to the docks of London during the bombing raids and found an old lady sitting outside her ruined cottage. Winston said, "Well, my dear, and how do you manage with the bombs?" And she said, "Oh, well, they do take your mind off the bloody war."

GABRIEL KOLKO: The dilemma the United States confronts in Vietnam is that the Vietnamese are not waiting to be slaughtered; they are fighting back, effectively and with a remarkable degree of efficiency that is probably unparalleled in the history of warfare. No matter what the United States wishes to do—even if it is willing to spend $60 billion a year on the war—the Vietnamese will resist. So far as the process of committing genocide is concerned, therefore, the United States has probably attained its maximum level of expenditure at this point in the war and is not likely to surpass the present level of destruction of the Vietnamese population. It is true, of course, that the United States could employ atomic technology in a random way, but that would only destroy the entire area, friend and foe alike, and serve no useful political purpose.

The war crime in Vietnam is the war itself. Apart from questions of individual guilt, it is the war, rather than the effects of the war that are an inherent part of it, which must be the main focus of any effort to stop war crimes.

JONATHAN SCHELL: There is a sense in which our technology and our enormous wealth makes this war possible. This is perhaps the first war ever fought in which defeat is impossible for one side—for our side. We cannot be defeated in the classical sense: The Vietcong are not going to take over our country or kick us into the sea.

What is possible and what occurs continuously is failure, repeated and continuous failure. But this is the first time that a country has had the resources to continue in a war in which it is continuously failing. Because of our incredible technology of war, we can go on and on with something that isn't working. We couldn't have done that just twenty years ago.

In the past a kind of law of survival was in operation. If you destroyed the civilian population of the country you were fighting, this had an effect on your own men, because the troops, to a considerable extent, had to live off the countryside. But we live completely by pipeline. I had calculated, for example, that we import more beer and soft drinks into South Vietnam every year than the enemy imports war matériel from the North.

Our failure, therefore, does not subject us to the classic pressures of exhaustion and lack of matériel, and because those pressures are not brought to bear, we can stay on indefinitely. The only thing that can drive us out is our recognition of the failure.

EDWARD M. OPTON, JR.: We need to take another look at the technology and bureaucracy that have been mentioned so often as causes of the escalated savagery of America's role in Vietnam. Both advanced technology and swollen bureaucracy *are* important, but it would be a terrible mistake to focus only on these factors, which we can do nothing about, when there are other channels through which we can exert our influence.

There is no doubt that America's technical triumphs in advanced machinery for butchering humans have contributed a great deal to the horror of Vietnam. However, it is equally important that many of the American war crimes in Vietnam are carried out with distinctly old-fashioned tools: pistols, knives, matches, field telephone electric magnetos attached to the genitals, and so forth. Moreover, neither the old nor the new tools of war are being used to their fullest extent in Vietnam. When I talked with American soldiers and officers in Vietnam, one of their most common complaints was, "We are fighting this war with one hand tied behind our back." Often they were quite bitter about it, and, in a grotesque sense, they had a point.

We have the technology easily to carry out a "final solution" to the Vietnam problem. We have made an excellent start on it, having forcibly displaced a very large proportion of the Vietnamese people from their homes, a crime that Hitler had not yet perpetrated on the Jews as late as 1938. But we have not committed a final solution—yet. If we do, the solution will take the form not of bringing the people to the ovens but of bringing the ovens to the people in the form of shiny, bright, aluminum napalm cylinders.

Among soldiers I interviewed in Vietnam, many felt that a final solution was the best and perhaps only solution, and many of their officers agreed. Extermination of the Vietnamese people, some officers felt, would be the best way to protect the men under them. No officer likes to see his "boys" go home in boxes.

But those who would use our technology to enforce a final solution have not been permitted to prevail—yet.

If one looks beyond the technological potentials in Vietnam, one sees that a macabre balance has been struck between terror and restraint. Because that balance represents only the leverage of opposing political forces and not any logical moral or military rationale, the balance could shift. The shift could be toward withdrawal, or it could be to the final solution.

The extent to which technology is used is a matter of what people can get away with. The practices of war are affected little by Geneva Conventions, but are affected profoundly by what each military commander—and the entire Government—can get away with at a particular time. In Vietnam, the men who would like to carry out a final solution have not been able to get away with it—yet.

They have been restrained by forces in our society, forces as real as technology and ultimately more powerful.

Bureaucracy has been the other bugaboo of this discussion. In a faceless organization no one can be held accountable. The blame is passed from private to lieutenant to captain to general and back down again. In theory the buck stops with the President, but in war crimes such as My Lai it actually is sloughed off from one level of the bureaucracy to another, and regardless of what a court-martial may decide, it will be impossible in justice to fix the responsibility on any one individual. When no one is accountable for a crime, crime does pay. War crimes are paying off daily in promotions for managers at all levels of the U.S. bureaucracy of death.

I think it would be foolish to act as if the end of colonial wars must wait for the rehumanization of bureaucracies. That might be a very long wait. Rather, we should look out for other aspects of modern life that might serve to counter the irresponsible, deadly hand of authoritarian bureaucracy. I will mention two such factors. One is the consciousness by many Americans that faraway peoples with dark skins, strange languages, and stranger customs are humans like ourselves, that they are people to be identified with, that they, too, should have the right to life, liberty, and the pursuit of happiness. This is a relatively new development in American history. If the war in Vietnam were being fought in the same totally racist atmosphere as the campaigns to exterminate the American Indians, the Vietnamese people would already have suffered the same fate as the native Americans. If the Vietnam war were fought even in the racial atmosphere that prevailed as recently as World War II, when we removed the Japanese-Americans to concentration camps in the desert, General Curtis LeMay would no doubt by now have been permitted to turn the countryside of Vietnam into a lawful and orderly parking lot. It is important that today most

Americans decisively reject that Teddy Roosevelt–General LeMay outlook on the world's other peoples. There is still room for hope.

A second factor that may yet block our irresponsible military-industrial complex is the technologically improved communication and still relatively free speech we enjoy in America. A discussion such as this one at the Capitol called by dissident Congressmen is still possible. Most important, a good many of the nasty facts of the war have been allowed to intrude into public view, even onto television. I doubt the propagandists who rallied the American people around the flag for earlier imperial wars could have imagined that a situation so dangerous to their interests would be allowed to develop.

It seems to me likely that factors like these—decreased racism and increased knowledge—account for the restraints that have so far held back our unlimited destructive potential. It is these factors—the factors we *can* do something about—that give us some thread of hope, however slender, that we ought to analyze most carefully.

Finding grounds for hope is most important. We have no lack of cogent analyses showing how the nature of technology, the nature of American society, and the nature of the war make massive war crimes inevitable. This is the Manifest Destiny doctrine upside down—still manifestly inevitable, but a signal for distress. If we find America's destiny to be irresistibly imperialist, then it is only logical to blow up buildings or blow up our minds with one drug or another. If there is no hope, why not? I believe we need not talk ourselves into such despair. There are grounds for hope, and we should have the courage to seek out those grounds and cultivate them.

III

AMERICANS
IN VIETNAM:

The Lessons of My Lai

"My Lai epitomizes the Vietnam war not only because every returning soldier can tell of similar incidents, if on a somewhat smaller scale, but also because it is an expression of the psychological state characteristic for Americans fighting that war. It illustrates the murderous progression of deception and self-deception—from political policy to military tactics to psychological aberration."

—ROBERT JAY LIFTON

ROBERT JAY LIFTON: The war in Vietnam has involved Americans in a malignant spiral of self-deception, brutalization, and numbing. Contradictions surrounding our intervention contribute directly to the brutalization of our troops; their indiscriminate killing of Vietnamese not only decimates that society and its people but reverberates back to the mother country and throughout the world; our leaders in turn are required to move more deeply into illusion and encourage similar illusion on the part of the American people; and *our* entire society undergoes a form of disintegration from which it may take decades to recover, if it is to recover at all. I would like to say something about each of these turns of the spiral.

Our policy in Vietnam is based upon three myths. The first of these concerns the nature of the war, and converts a forty-five-year-old anticolonial revolution into an "outside invasion" of the South by the North. The second myth concerns the nature of the government we support, and converts a despotic military regime without standing among its own people into a "democratic ally." The third myth holds that we can "Vietnamize" the war—leave and still keep the present government in power in the South —by turning it over to a regime that lacks legitimacy and an army that has shown little will to fight—by a program that is American rather than Vietnamese and one that few if any Vietnamese really want to implement. It is common knowledge among those who have been in Vietnam recently that most South Vietnamese in government (and in the military below the rank of major or colonel) tend to be opposed to the war. Many among them have interests and even loyalties somewhere on the Left. Those in the higher ranks who have an interest in continuing the war could not permit Vietnamization to succeed, because they could not sustain their power if the Americans were to leave.

The massacre at My Lai is a product of our self-deception. By no means an outgrowth of the ordinary stresses of war, My Lai is the result of a psychological state created by specific features of the war in Vietnam. Americans fighting that war are intruders in an Asian revolution, and become profoundly confused by their inability to distinguish the enemy from the people. Their anger at allies who do not fight, and who seem to be part of an environment of general deterioration, becomes readily converted into racist perceptions of the Vietnamese as nonpeople. Such perceptions are furthered by our military policy of compensating for our "blindness" by saturating the environment with our technology of destruction, thereby conveying to the GI the sense that Vietnamese are expendable. Seeing their buddies killed, but finding themselves unable to take revenge upon or even locate the adversary, GIs experience a desperate need to find an enemy who can be made to stand still. Their diffuse rage against all Vietnamese can lead to something close to an illusion that, by gunning down little babies and women and old men, they have finally "engaged" the enemy—can lead, in other words, to My Lai.

My Lai thus epitomizes the Vietnam war not only because every returning combat soldier can tell of similar incidents, if on a somewhat smaller scale, but also because it is an expression of the psychological state characteristic for Americans fighting that war. It illustrates the murderous progression of deception and self-deception—from political policy to military tactics to psychological aberration. The Vietnamese people are, of course, the victims, with American GIs caught in the middle and rendered both victims and executioners.

Turning now to the rest of the American population and its response to My Lai, we can identify at least three psychological mechanisms called forth to avoid facing such unpleasant truths. The first is denial: "The massacres didn't really happen or have been exaggerated." The second is rationalization: "All war is hell." And the third, in a way more politically dangerous, is the mobilization of self-righteous anger: "Stop picking on our boys. The Vietnamese had it coming to them. You [the bearer of the news] ought to be sent to Vietnam to fight." This has actually been the response received by one leading television commentator from large numbers of viewers who called in after he broadcast interviews with GIs who had participated in these massacres.

We know something about the ways in which groups and even nations refuse to feel their own atrocities. We have the experience of Nazi Germany for that, and many other experiences. But I would stress that in so doing in this case, in refusing to feel not only My Lai but the entire Vietnam war, we partake precisely in the psychic numbing and brutalization experienced by GIs, even if indirectly and in less extreme form.

Our numbing and brutalization are furthered and hardened by the insistence on the part of our leaders that My Lai is no more than an isolated incident in a war that will be solved, at least for us, by Vietnamization.

The paradox here is that many of these same leaders would like to take us out of Vietnam but are prevented from doing so by the self-deceptions contained within their world view. They are bound by a cosmology that contrasts absolute American purity with absolute Communist depravity. Also contained in this cosmology is a dangerous form of technicism that leads Americans to view Vietnam (or Vietnamization) as no more than "a job to be done" through the application of "American know-how," and to ignore psychological and historical forces surrounding the long-standing Vietnamese struggle against Western invaders.

The cost of this American self-deception to the Vietnamese people has become grotesquely clear. But there is no way of measuring its mounting cost to our own society. What we can say is that Americans as a national group have become participants in, and survivors of, a sustained pattern of killing and dying which we inwardly sense to be not only brutal but ultimately absurd. That is, the larger American population shares the experience of Vietnam combat veterans in being unable to find the inner significance that any survivor requires in relationship to his death immersion. Our own justifications for our actions convince us incompletely, if at all, and we are left with the numbing and brutalization required to protect those justifications and fend off a sense of guilt. We are already experiencing the consequences of this general process, and our psychological scars are likely to be extensive and permanent.

It is no secret that a very large percentage of our most gifted young people feel betrayed and victimized—by the war, by our political leaders, by the older generation, and by our society in general. What we are now learning is that large numbers of Vietnam veterans bring back into that society a similar but more painfully concrete sense of betrayal and victimization, of having been used badly, sacrificed without purpose, by their country. Again these emotions extend throughout the American population: Everyone feels in some way betrayed and victimized—either by the war and its advocates, or by those who oppose the war and raise the specter of defeat.

Even without the war it is quite possible that the general dislocations and antagonisms in our society would have eventually led to considerable violence. But desperate emotions in response to the war escalate the possibilities for violence from all sides: from returning GIs who can neither absorb their experience nor rid themselves of the habit of killing; from the young who are enraged by their country's demand that they participate in evil forms of killing and dying; from blacks who associate this war against a nonwhite race with their own sense of racial oppression; and, most dangerous of all, from backlash-prone groups throughout American society who cling nostalgically to their cosmology and feel not only betrayed and victimized by protesters but duped by leaders who promised them a brief war and a glorious victory.

Self-deception, moreover, tends to expand to other realms, and this expansion could be accelerated by the need to deny its existence in regard to Vietnam. Hence the danger of other Vietnams occurring in Southeast Asia, Latin America, or elsewhere, and the apocalyptic prospect of similarly spreading self-deception in the Faustian area of nuclear weapons systems. In that area a little numbing and a little self-deception, even in the absence of brutalization, could mean the extinction of virtaully everyone.

Clearly, our task is to break out of this malignant spiral. We cannot do so through detached psychological—or, for that matter, economic or political—analysis. Rather, we must commit ourselves to precisely what our leaders are failing to do: We must confront events like My Lai by reporting them as accurately as we can and interpreting them with whatever wisdom we possess. We must convey the full story of what has been going on in Vietnam, not by simply inundating the American people with grotesque details and thereby mobilizing their resistance to the truth, but by giving *form* to these details and events within the larger context of the Vietnam war and its causes. We must also take actions, both forceful and wise, that express our absolute opposition to the national policies and directions which have brought us to this point. Finally, we must evolve and act upon a new world view —a very different cosmology—that reaches beyond My Lai and Vietnam and beyond our present political and military policies and structures.

As a citizen, and as a psychiatrist working in the field of psychohistory, I fear for my country. We are in the midst of a national crisis of unique historical and psychological dimensions. My Lai is no more than the top of the iceberg—or to return to my original image, it is just one turn of the spiral. But we had better face My Lai if we are going to unwind that malignant spiral, cease our destruction of Vietnamese and American societies, and apply ourselves to the larger problem of human survival.

HANS MORGENTHAU: I do not agree with the proposition that the massacre at My Lai is the result of self-deception. It is the logical consequence of the enterprise in which we are engaged. For if you are engaged in a war directed not against a distinguishable army, not against a particular group within a population, but against the population as a whole, it becomes perfectly logical—perfectly rational, I would even say—to regard every man, woman, and child as an actual or potential enemy who has to be eliminated. So I am firmly convinced that what happened in My Lai and elsewhere were not accidents, or deviations created by self-deception, but the inevitable outgrowth of the kind of war we are waging.

ROBERT JAY LIFTON: My point was simply that the political illusions lead directly to psychological illusions on the part of our troops in Vietnam or, putting the matter more strongly, that political madness leads to behavioral madness. It is a very direct relationship.

Consider what Sergeant Michael Bernhardt, the man who did not fire at My Lai, has said about this: "You know, when I think of somebody who would shoot up women and children, I think of a real nut, a real maniac, a real psycho, somebody who's just completely lost control and doesn't have any idea of what he's doing. That's what I figured. That's what I thought a nut was. Then I found out that an act like, you know, murder for no reason could be done by just about anybody." What that reveals is that in a certain kind of extreme environment moral standards are totally reversed, and, as Professor Morgenthau said, what has been sane becomes psychotic and what has been psychotic becomes sane.

JONATHAN SCHELL: The war in Vietnam has a dream-like quality—not simply because it is happening on television, but because like a dreamer we face a reality that is of our own creation. Although a dreamer may be surprised or shocked by what he encounters in the dream, those surprises have been authored by himself. In the same way, we have imposed definitions on Vietnam that have created the reality we face.

When we go into a village, for example, we classify all the people into different categories. But these categories do not depend on something we perceive about them; they depend on what we do to them. If we kill them, they are Vietcong. If we capture them and tie them up, they are Vietcong suspects. If we grab them and move them to a camp, they are hostile civilians. Having done this to many people who were in fact innocent, the definitions we have imposed become real. The men who have been tied up or tortured actually become our enemies and shoot real bullets at us, but still we are facing the shadow of our own actions.

EDWARD M. OPTON, JR.:* Revelation of the My Lai massacre caused widespread initial shock and bewilderment. The public, the press, and our colleagues have found this event very difficult to comprehend. War crimes are not something we have associated with Americans. The psychological tension caused by the poor fit between the facts and the expectations Americans have of themselves makes it possible that out of the charnel heap we may learn some lessons about ourselves. But if anything is to be learned, social scientists will have to have the moral courage to learn and to teach.

We claim no unique knowledge about My Lai, but we do believe that facts long on record permit some reasonably certain elementary conclusions:

*This statement is adapted from papers by Dr. Opton and two of his associates at the Wright Institute, Nevitt Sanford and Robert Duckles, which appeared in somewhat different form in the February 21, 1970, issue of *The New Republic* and the March, 1970, issue of *Trans-Action.*

1. *Most of the explanations that have been advanced are seriously lacking in credibility. They explain away rather than explain; they say in one way or another that My Lai doesn't really count rather than acknowledge its significance.*

Almost all public speculation on the massacre has begun with the assumption that it was an isolated, uncharacteristic incident. The speculation therefore has been on what exceptional circumstances could have resulted in such a deviation from normality. "They must have gone berserk" is the most oversimplified of these kinds of speculation.

Explanations in terms of the hard fighting and casualties the men had experienced fall into this category. The facts are that many units have fought harder and longer, suffered more casualties, and lived under worse conditions than Company C, 1st Battalion, 20th Infantry, both in this and other wars. Uncomfortable and dangerous as the war in Vietnam is for our men, it is a great deal less uncomfortable and a great deal less dangerous for the typical soldier than the Korean war or World Wars I and II.

Efforts to find an explanation of the massacre in the personalities of the officers and enlisted men involved are similarly misdirected. Undoubtedly these men have their quirks and oddities, but so do all of us. No one has reported behavior of the officers or enlisted men before or after My Lai that smacks of abnormality. Parents of the men have rarely complained that their sons returned from Vietnam in any abnormal psychic state. The men are reported to have gone about their gruesome work for the most part with cool efficiency and tragic effectiveness. The fact that the accused officers and men did nothing to draw special attention to themselves in the months before and after the massacre indicates that they were not remarkably different from the run-of-the-mill soldier. Genuine explanations of My Lai will require us to pay attention to the factors that lead ordinary men to do extraordinary things. The

American tradition is to locate the source of evil deeds in
evil men. We have yet to learn that the greatest evils occur
when social systems give average men the task of routiniz-
ing evil.

Another kind of speculation on the causes of My Lai is
the reverse of those discussed above. "This kind of thing
happens in war," it is said. "It's terrible, but you have to
expect excesses in combat." Not so. There have been excesses in combat in every war, but we know of no direct
parallel to the My Lai massacre by American troops in any
recent war except the war in Vietnam. Many of the restraints Americans applied to themselves in other wars
have been dropped in this one. American troops characteristically have not lined up old men, old women, moth-
ers, children, and babies in front of ditches and shot them
down. The massacre is most emphatically *not* the "kind of
thing that happens" in recent American wars. The question for investigation is: In what ways is My Lai the kind
of thing that is done as a matter of routine in Vietnam?

The pattern of violence at My Lai does not resemble a
riot or a mass psychosis. But it does have its counterparts
in certain American traditions: genocidal attacks on
American Indians in the nineteenth century and mass
lynchings which persisted until the 1930s. Scientific studies of lynch mobs have shown that the members of such
mobs are by no means berserk; rather, theirs is an all-too-
rational response to the encouragement, spoken or un-
spoken, of their community leaders. The attitudes of
elected officials and leading members of the community
are crucial in permitting lynchings; rarely if ever has a
mob carried out a lynching when the community leadership truly opposed it. It is important that at My Lai, as at
the mass lynchings of blacks and the genocide of the native Americans, the victims were of a different race.

2. *The most important fact about the My Lai massacre
is that it was only a minor step beyond the standard,*

official, routine U.S. policy in Vietnam.

It is official U.S. policy in Vietnam to obliterate not just whole villages, but whole districts and virtually whole provinces. At first, efforts were made to remove the inhabitants before "saving" the regions by destroying them, but the pressure of the vast numbers of refugees thus created—at least one-quarter of the entire rural population of South Vietnam—has led to policies even more genocidal. Jonathan and Orville Schell have told how Army units in Quang Ngai province were ordered not to "generate" any more refugees when "pacification camps" became full. The Army complied, continuing its search-and-destroy operations but no longer issuing warnings to peasants before air strikes were called in on their villages. Every civilian on the ground was assumed to be enemy by the pilots. Air strikes on civilians became a matter of routine.

The genocidal policy is carried out in other ways as well. I have personally accompanied a routine operation in which U.S. Cobra helicopters fired 20mm. cannons into the houses of a typical village in territory controlled by the National Liberation Front. They also shot the villagers who ran out of the houses. This was termed "prepping the area" by the American lieutenant colonel who directed the operation. "We sort of shoot it up to see if anything moves," he explained, and he added by way of reassurance that this treatment was perfectly routine.

It is official U.S. policy to establish "free-fire zones" and "kill zones" where anything that moves is fired upon. Although in the original theory these were zones from which civilians had been removed, it has long been well known that free-fire zones now include many inhabited villages. It is official U.S. policy to destroy the Vietnamese people's stockpiles of rice in N.L.F.-influenced areas, thus starving the women and children (the armed men, we may be sure, provide themselves with the undestroyed portion of the rice harvest), and it is official, though secret, U.S. policy to destroy rice and other crops with chemical defoliants.

Official U.S. policy long ago gave up the idea of gaining the allegiance of the people of Vietnam. "Winning the hearts and minds" is now maintained only as a public relations product for consumption on the home market. In Vietnam itself the policy is, as explained by a U.S. Marine officer, "If you've got them by the balls, the hearts and minds will follow." Getting the villagers by the balls means bombing and shelling them from their villages, assassinating their leaders, breaking up their families by removing the men, and removing the rural population to concentration camps euphemistically called "refugee camps." All these official policies involve killing, and killing on a large scale. It is routine policy to talk about what we are doing only in euphemisms like "population control," "prepping the area," and so forth. And it is standard practice to talk about the Vietnamese people in depersonalized terms like "gooks," "slopes," and "dinks." This makes it easier to kill civilians—knowingly, routinely, and massively.

The euphemisms and the depersonalization may enable headquarters personnel, the politicans above them, and the American public to pretend that large-scale killing of civilians does not occur, but the troops in the field know better. The furor over the My Lai massacre must have seemed to them grimly illogical. As the satirist Art Hoppe put it, "The best way [to kill civilians], it's generally agreed, is to kill them with bombs, rockets, artillery shells, and napalm. Those who kill women and children in these ways are called heroes. . . ." How is it, the foot soldier must wonder, that "to kill women and children at less than 500 paces is an atrocity; at more than 500 paces, it's an act of heroism."

The official policy that results in large-scale killing of

civilians through impersonal, long-distance weapons is matched by an official practice of inaction to reduce the cumulatively large-scale killing of civilians in thousands of individual, personal atrocities: dropping civilians out of helicopters and killing civilians by torture during interrogations; picking off civilians in their rice paddies in the large areas where anything that moves is "officially" considered an enemy; killing civilians for sport; "plinking" at them from passing air and land vehicles; and so on. These small-scale war crimes have become so common that our reporters have stopped reporting them; they are no longer "news." They have become routine to many of our soldiers, too, and the soldiers, to preserve their equilibrium, have developed the classical psychological methods of justifying what they see happening. The soldier comes to think of the Vietnamese not as human like himself, but as something less than human. It is only a small further step to the conclusion that "the only good dink is a dead dink," as Specialist 4 James Farmer, Company C, Fourth Battalion, Third Infantry, 198th Infantry Brigade, Americal Division, expressed it to *The New York Times.*

The foot soldier in Vietnam sees Specialist Farmer's conclusion acted out daily, by air, by artillery, by quick death in a napalm holocaust, by slow death in a foodless, waterless refugee camp, and by the unpunished examples of his fellow soldiers cutting down a civilian here, a family there. "The only good dink is a dead dink" is in the wind in Vietnam, and our soldiers receive plenty of training in bending before the wind of the Army way of doing things. In that official and quasi-official "climate," the My Lai massacre logically represents no major deviation. The massacre was a minor embellishment on established policy and practice. We believe it would be hypocritical self-righteousness to condemn the men who committed a minor embellishment without condemning those who set the criminal policy itself.

3. *The major responsibility and guilt for the massacre lies with the elected officials who make U.S. policy in Vietnam and with the high military officials who have misled both elected officials and the general public as to what they have been doing under the name of those policy directives.*

Our elected officials and their appointed advisers have special knowledge and considerable freedom of choice, and they have taken it upon themselves to act as our leaders. We therefore have the right and the duty to hold them personally responsible for the ignorance, insensibility, lack of human understanding, and poor judgment they have displayed in shaping our Vietnam policy. Especially deserving of blame are those officials who knew that policies were wrong but found it expedient to remain silent rather than endanger their careers or risk the ill will of their "teammates." This, discouragingly enough, might hold for the great majority of Senators who voted for the Tonkin Gulf Resolution. The very one-sidedness of that vote was enough to indicate that Senators were not using their heads in our behalf but were more or less automatically displaying their anti-Communist valor. That vote by itself was clear evidence that we were embarking on a "crusade" of the totally good, peace-loving people—ourselves—against the totally evil.

A psychologist might say that crusaders like John Foster Dulles and Dean Rusk were prisoners of their narrow Protestant upbringings or that they merely expressed in their actions the prevailing American ethnocentrism, but this does not excuse their failure to learn from experience or their apparent inability to think of anything to do about Communism save to imitate its worst features.

There is ample evidence that high officials in our government have participated fully in the practice of portraying the "other side" as an aggregate of evil demons. This imagery has become so prominent and routine in official pronouncements and in the media that only people with some determination to think for themselves can resist adopting it as a matter of course. Among high officials, as among the general public, the dehumanization of "the enemy" tends to spread, so that now those who dare to demonstrate against our Vietnam policy are called by the Vice President "parasites," "goats," and "creeps."

The implications of public utterances like those of the Vice President are not far to seek. "I think," a nineteen-year-old infantryman told a reporter, "someone ought to kill those long-haired, queer bastards back in the world. Anyone who demonstrates against the war ought to be lined up and killed, just like any gook here." I know from personal experience that this is not an uncommon sentiment.

4. *America's citizens share in the responsibility for My Lai, for there has been available to all ample evidence that the United States has been committing large-scale war crimes in Vietnam. A will to disbelieve, a self-serving reluctance to know the truth, just plain indifference, as well as failings in our ethics and our educational system, have prevented our electorate from influencing politicians whose policies allow for crimes against humanity.*

If some of us are disposed to blame our elected officials for wrong policies in Vietnam, these officials are quick enough to pass the responsibility back to the general public, pointing to opinion polls and silent majorities that favor these policies. These officials have a good point. We as a people do bear much of the responsibility for My Lai. The guilt is in large part collective. It can certainly be argued that the massacre would not have happened had our soldiers not been brought up in a culture in which racism and a good-versus-evil, Manichean approach to international relations are deeply rooted. It is quite possible that a large number, perhaps a critically larger number, of the soldiers would have refused to take part in the massacre had they not been raised on a psychic diet of television violence, which almost every day of their lives impressed its lesson of the cheapness of life. Few of us, social scientists or not, have done much that was personally inconvenient to discover or to fight against either the root sources or the proximal causes of My Lai. Yet the case is certainly different with those citizens who have opposed the war than it is with those who favored it; and those who have reluctantly given assent are in a diffrent psychological situation than those who have participated vicariously in the killing and the "victories." There are, in other words, different degrees of actual responsibility and of potentiality for feelings of guilt.

Some light is shed on these matters by a survey of reaction to My Lai carried out by students and staff members of the Wright Institute in December, 1969. As far as we know, this was the first study ever attempted on American response to alleged American war crimes. Our conclusion: The same impetus to an emotional cop-out that produces complacent members of a silent majority is surprisingly strong in almost all of us, young as well as old, liberal as well as conservative, interviewer as well as interviewee.

Our sample was not a large one—most of our data came from forty-two long interviews with randomly selected telephone subscribers in Oakland, California, plus four in-person interviews—but the results are consistent with larger, less intensive surveys by *The Wall Street Journal, The Minneapolis Tribune,* and *Time. Time* reported that 65 per cent of its sample of 1,608 individuals denied being upset by the news of the alleged massacre. Our intensive interviews throw some light on how those 65 per cent assimilate My Lai to the expected, normal routine of things, or disbelieve that any massacre took place, or do both simultaneously.

Anyone who would understand how people defuse the potential emotional chaos that would logically follow from knowledge of monstrous atrocities committed in their name must begin with the Germans. In the years following 1945 the Allies carried out an active Denazification program which included massive attempts to educate the German people about what they and their government had done. On the theory that a Germany ignorant of its history would be condemned to repeat it, the Allies tried to make Germans aware of Nazi war crimes and German guilt. The effort was a failure. Our propagandists found that it is almost impossible to induce people to think about what they prefer to forget. With few exceptions, Germans interviewed during the Denazification campaign stood at a far emotional distance from the Nazi crimes, feeling personally and morally uninvolved and unconcerned, or they denied the facts, or they projected the guilt on others, or they rationalized and justified the atrocities, or they simultaneously engaged in several or all of these mental maneuvers, little inhibited by logical consistency.

Americans react similarly to the news of their alleged war crimes. A young airline stewardess showed most clearly how emotion is suppressed. During the interview she was asked to inspect the *Life* magazine photographs of My Lai. As she viewed the mangled bodies and the contorted faces of those about to die she trembled and her chin dropped to her chest. Her eyes closed to shut the pictures out. For several seconds she seemed unable to move. But she recovered immediately, for we then asked: "You said before that you weren't surprised. Do you have any other reactions besides that?" She responded: "No, I don't. . . . It . . . when people are taught to hate it doesn't surprise me how they react, particularly when they are given a weapon; it just seems to be one of the outcomes of war. . . ."

Some people put the role of suppression of emotion, and the rationalizations that make emotional uninvolvement possible, even more clearly. One said: "I can't take the responsibility of the world on my shoulders too strongly myself.... It upsets me. I'm having my problems and can't take this stuff too seriously, since it causes me worries and problems."

Another person, one who refused to be interviewed, said: "Well, I don't know, you see, I can't get upset about all these things, so I can't give you an opinion one way or the other. Okay?"

Partial or complete denial of the fact of the alleged massacre at My Lai was common. One might expect the extreme forms of denial from such people as Staff Sergeant David Mitchell, one of the accused, who has said: "I can recall no such case where I know of anyone being hurt.... It is my opinion that what they say happened did not happen." And one might expect the same reaction from former Alabama Governor George Wallace: "I can't believe an American serviceman would purposely shoot any civilian.... Any atrocities in this war were caused by the Communists." But total denial is by no means confined to those implicated in the alleged massacre and to super-patriots. A man who felt that the U.S. should, but cannot, get out of Vietnam told us: "Our boys wouldn't do this. Something else is behind it."

Another complete denial came from a woman who, like the man above, was ambivalent about the war. At one moment she advocated withdrawal by the end of 1970; however, she also endorsed the idea of escalating and winning the war, no matter what the consequences, *but* without killing innocent people. As for My Lai, she said: "It's too unbelievable that they would do something like that." Another person, asked if he believed the massacre really happened, first gave a strong endorsement of President Nixon's policy, then said: "I can't really and truly. No. I don't. I think it could have been a prefabricated story by a bunch of losers."

Strong doubts served the same purpose as complete

denial for some people. "Anything could happen. How do we know what's going on?" asked a man who wanted the war escalated, and one of several individuals who felt so threatened by the subject that they cut off the interview in the middle said: "No, sometimes I don't [believe that the massacre happened]. Sometimes I think that our newspapermen get a little bit wild." Implicit in the words of some respondents seemed to be a plea, a real desire to find a way not to have to believe in the reality of the alleged massacre. A sixty-six-year-old grandmother described her family's reaction: "My foster daughter doesn't believe it. She thinks it never happened. Finally [she] admitted to me that she doesn't want to believe it happened. She doesn't want to believe it. She knows in her heart but refuses to face facts."

Justification was the other most prevalent means of coping with the unwelcome news. One of the principal justifications our respondents offered was the idea that orders must be followed. Even some of the more dovish respondents gave statements like this: "What would their punishment have been if they had disobeyed? Do they get shot if they don't shoot someone else?" And another "moderate" dove said: "They were given an order to do something. They will shoot you if you don't. They had no choice."

Only a few respondents recalled that some of the GIs *had* refused to shoot. One of those few was asked what the men should have done. He said: "What a lot of them did, refuse. Quite a few of them refused. Fact is, I even read where one of them shot himself in the foot so he would be evacuated, so he wouldn't have any part of it."

The idea that one must follow orders was more acceptable to men than to women; when asked what they personally would have done if ordered to line up people and kill them, 74 per cent of women said they would have refused, but only 27 per cent of men. Perhaps ominously, youth were no more independent of spirit than their elders; those over thirty-six more often favored putting the enlisted men who did the shooting on trial than did those under thirty-six, and slightly more of the older group expressly said that the men should have disobeyed orders to kill civilians.

The idea that the men were justified by the orders they received implies a projection of guilt to somewhere higher up, and a number of our respondents made this explicit. Germans, similarly, tended to blame the German war crimes on Hitler, their leaders, the National Socialist party, the S.S., or on military fanatics. But the idea that Germans, as individuals, might have been in turn responsible for selection and toleration of their leaders was steadfastly rejected. While the question of responsibility lying with the American public was not specifically asked of our predominantly dovish sample, *no one extended the scope of responsibility to himself in particular or the American people in general.* It is encouraging, however, that in a follow-up questionnaire three months later several respondents did say they believed Americans, including themselves, were ultimately responsible for My Lai.

Another popular justification was the idea that the alleged victims were not really civilians, but enemies: "Now had these civilians, had these women set booby traps for these people?" Another man who felt he was a dove ("I'd hate to say I'm a hawk"), yet who advocated that the U.S. should "let out the stops," said, "These little bastards are devious," implying in context that the women and children were not really innocent bystanders.

None of the respondents *said* that My Lai was justified as revenge for N.L.F. actions, but many seemed to *think* so: "I understand that the Vietcong, from the start, have bombed schoolyards, schoolhouses, movie theaters, restaurants . . . just worthless bombing, and it's killing innocent people by the score. And these are their own people." And a hawk said: "Our boys have been castrated by the VC and no one stood up for them. There was no sensation made of this."

The various ways of defusing the emotional potential of My Lai were used by hawks and doves alike, though not in equal proportions. Hawks, more than others, tended to justify the alleged massacre. Both hawks and doves argued in one way or another no massacre happened. The doves tended to comfort themselves with the thought that My Lai's happen in every war, hence they need not be upset. Regardless of the method, the effect was the same: emotional disengagement. We believe the general nonresponse to My Lai by our random sample of Oaklanders was not fundamentally different from the nonresponse of Kitty Genovese's neighbors, who heard her protracted screams and cries for help as she was slowly murdered, but who declined to get involved, and who reported afterwards a similar, seemingly paradoxical, emotional detachment. Whether it is Vietnamese peasants or one's next-door neighbor, emotional detachment makes it possible to keep one's attention and concern focused on Number One, me, myself, I. No malignant evil intent is necessary for men to tolerate or even reluctantly to applaud war crimes; all that is required is self-centeredness. This focus on the self need not imply any pathological egotism, but only alienated impotence to effect the course of events. Milton Mayer explained the phenomenon in his analysis of the Germans' passive acceptance of Nazism: "Responsible men never shirk responsibility and so, when they must reject it, they deny it. They draw the curtain. They detach themselves altogether from the consideration of the evil they ought to, but cannot, contend with. Their denial compels their detachment."

5. *Little is to be gained, and perhaps much lost, by attempts to force recognition of responsibility on those who now completely wash their hands of the blood of My*

Lai. But if we were to assume that no one can be stirred to action by such atrocities, or if we fail to press for full and frank application of social science to American war crimes, we would participate by passivity in the horror of America's My Lai's, past and future.

We must make sure that as many people as possible know the truth and are guided by it. Unless a substantial number of people who can speak and write with authority strive to keep the evil of My Lai's, and of the larger policy of which it is an expression, before the public, it is difficult to see what will prevent our military from persisting in genocide in Vietnam and in future Vietnams.

But dealing with this guilt-laden subject will not be easy, for guilt that is on the edge of consciousness can lead to further destructiveness more easily than to contrition. Charles Manson, the alleged leader of the group accused of the Sharon Tate murders, seeing that his followers were shaken after their night's work, reportedly insisted that they commit more murders the next night. This psychological stratagem was used regularly in the Nazis' training of the S.S. Efforts to induce consciousness of guilt in people who lack the inner strength to bear it can backfire, evoking behavior that relieves queasiness by demonstrating that what is feared can be done, even more and worse, without catastrophic consequences to oneself.

Public breast-beating, whether self-flagellation or condemnation of everyone except oneself, is probably futile at best and a dangerous indulgence at worst. Constructive handling of feelings about My Lai will require attention to what we can do to prevent future atrocities, to end the Vietnam war, and to block the next Vietnam.

Social scientists in particular need not be part of a silent majority as, with rare exceptions, we so far have been. Psychologists can make themselves heard in investigating what makes some killing psychologically "close" and shocking, while the same death by bomb or shell is a matter of indifference. Sociologists have not yet reported on the structural aspects of the military reward system that ensures that almost all war crimes remain unreported. Economists can calculate and publicize the enormous indirect costs of the war, such as disability pensions and survivor benefits that will continue into the twenty-first century. Historians could try to make the public aware of the nearly fatal effects of the Indochinese and Algerian wars on French democracy. Survey researchers, psychiatrists, and clinical psychologists could assay the extent of long-lasting alienation and anomie among returned Vietnam veterans. The social sciences could join together in examining the pervasive distortion in information as it passes up and down the chain of military and civilian command and how this distortion is used to justify and rationalize mass murder.

The psychology, sociology, economics, and history of colonial wars particularly deserve more attention. One of the most insidious arguments for continuation of the Vietnam war is the proposition that termination in less than victory would produce a massive political backlash. We would do well to study and to make much better known the French experience after the Algerian war and the British experience following their withdrawals from India and Suez. For that matter, it would be well to study some of our own retreats from political-military intervention abroad. Withdrawal from Vietnam would not make President Nixon the first American President to "lose a war," as he professedly fears, but this historical fact must be made a psychological reality if we are to extricate ourselves from the Vietnam morass. Coming out on the short end of a military conflict has not sapped the will, ruined the economy, or spoiled the society of the United States in the past; and these bugaboos, which are within the legitimate subject matter of the social sciences, need to be expunged from our minds. That will take work.

Funding such work will be difficult, but if social scientists think the work is important enough, they will find the means of sponsorship and support. There are times when to know and to remain silent is to be an accomplice. One of the lessons of My Lai is that silence in the face of such human disaster can no longer be an acceptable response.

ROBERT JAY LIFTON: I have talked to many returning GIs about their experience—their psychological experience —in Vietnam. No soldier I have talked to—and none of the two hundred or so that a friend and colleague and historian has talked to in his investigations—has ever been surprised by the news of My Lai. That is an interesting fact. They have not been surprised because they have either been party to, or witness to, or have heard fairly close-hand about hundreds or thousands of similar, if smaller, incidents. My Lai is outstanding, it would seem, only for its size.

One cannot separate policy from My Lai. A psychological state formed in Americans in pursuing the war in Vietnam leads directly to My Lai, and that psychological state if directly influenced by their witnessing larger military policies, such as the free-fire zones, where the Vietnamese become expendable.

DANIEL ELLSBERG: As a peacetime Marine in the 1950s, I was spared the need to confront the possibility that the enemies I was being trained to kill for my country might turn out to be women, children, and babies. I was surrounded then by people who had been in World War II and Korea, and I was trained on war stories of jungle fighting on isolated Pacific islands. These are the myths that have affected the attitudes of this generation of Americans toward violence. Vietnam, of course, has raised questions which this mythic history did not force us to confront—questions about who we are and what we are trying to do and what is permissible to us.

The first point I would like to raise about My Lai is this: If there were no My Lai's, no face-to-face killing of women and children by small arms, would the civilians of South Vietnam really know the difference? As you may have noticed, the South Vietnamese civilians, let alone their leadership, did not really raise much protest about My Lai or even show much interest in it. First of all, they are used to such operations in that area—particularly by Koreans, the allies we brought to Vietnam.

Moreover, it is hard for the South Vietnamese to get very excited about killings committed in that particular way, knowing that nearly all of the enormous number of civilian deaths are caused by high explosives from our planes and artillery. They have come to expect these deaths, the killing of women and children from a distance, as a part of the American way of war.

The question remains, how did this particular face-to-face massacre come about? Is it the nature of this war? Is it inevitable in this sort of war? These questions have all been raised. I would suggest that it is in the nature of this war and to be expected. This is the major reason I have concluded that the war in which I participated is one we should not have been fighting. But the cause, I would suggest, is not so much strategic or tactical in any objective sense, but psychological, in terms of the pressures that this war puts on those who participate in it. These pressures lead daily to smaller, unrecorded atrocities, but sooner or later they were likely to produce a My Lai.

The first thing to be mentioned is the frustration to both planners and soldiers of fighting in a war where nothing seems to work, where the rules either don't exist or obviously don't apply, and where they are confronted by impotence and failure day after day. My Lai had to be destroyed not because its occupants posed any threat, but because there was a felt need to destroy some village like it.

I saw that kind of frustration and the effects of it very vividly toward the close of my two years in Vietnam. I saw it develop in a short period—only ten days—in a particular battalion which had been fighting for some months in the jungles of War Zone C where there were no villages. Now the same battalion was exposed to the conditions of the Delta, surrounded by villages and surrounded by water—in fact immersed in water constantly, which added to the frustration. The men preferred the dry jungle fighting.

As days went on in which the men were fired at by invisible snipers, losing casualties at a considerable rate but never having the satisfaction of a body to add to their statistics or to give them evidence that they were having an effect, they grew increasingly angry. The only body they encountered in this ten-day period was that of an eighteen-year-old girl killed by a stray artillery shell.

At this point I took a very odd photograph of a soldier furiously bayoneting a canteen. His lieutenant had just asked for permission to burn an empty house that we had come to and were searching. Because it had this canteen in it and a picture of someone in a uniform that was not familiar to our troops, they assumed it was a Vietcong house and asked for permission to burn it. Permission was denied. There was much swearing and stamping around, and the soldiers took the offending canteen and punched it full of holes. Their desire to burn the house was in part the result of frustration and in part reflected the fact that they honestly didn't know what might work. They had the feeling that at least if they burned the houses, something would happen; their presence would have been marked. Perhaps the Vietcong would be discouraged from operating in that area, though there were many houses, thousands in the area, and unless you burned them all, the Vietcong would still have shelter.

A week later I was on a patrol that burned every house it came to. I assumed the orders had been changed. When I returned to the battalion headquarters, I asked the operations officer why he had changed the orders, but he denied they had been changed. I said, "You can see the smoke over there, can't you?" Pillars of smoke were rising. He replied, "Sure, I see that smoke. I called the company commander and asked him what the smoke was and he said they were burning the thatch off bunkers." I said, "They were burning every house they came to." He said he would do something about it. Within ten days this battalion had moved to a state of mind where lieutenants and captains were burning houses in violation of higher orders and lying about it.

The understanding of My Lai has been distorted in some accounts I have read by the suggestion that something like this probably happens all the time. This may be true, on a smaller scale, of the Koreans, but is not really quite true of our troops. My Lai was beyond the bounds of permissible behavior, and that is recognizable by virtually every soldier in Vietnam. They know it was wrong: No shots had been fired at the soldiers, no enemy troops were in the village, nobody was armed. The men who were at My Lai knew there were aspects out of the ordinary. That is why they tried to hide the event, talked about it to no one, discussed it very little even among themselves.

But if My Lai was still exceptional, it was separated only by a very fine distinction from incidents that occur regularly and that are regarded as permissible. A few shots from the village, a few uniforms found in a hut, a measure of resistance, would have removed any question about what happened at My Lai. We operate on the principle that any action is permissible against a foe—even if he is a thirteen-year-old boy who is carrying a rifle—or even, when we come to strategic bombing, against anyone whose death might inconvenience a foe.

I am reminded of the occasion of my first sight of an alleged enemy in Vietnam. I was flying over the Plain of Reeds with a pilot who had a deserved reputation for daring and acuity; he could spot fox holes and bunkers and what-not from a great height, long before I would have seen them. At one point in the flight he told me over the intercom, "There is a VC down there." At his suggestion, I had brought a weapon with me, in case we were shot down. As soon as he spoke, I drew my pistol. He pulled out his M16 rifle and went into a dive. I looked down and saw two men in black pajamas on the ground, apparently running away from a boat nearby. I noticed that they were not armed, and mentioned this to the pilot. He said he assumed they had left their weapons in the boat. He came down again, firing the M16 from the moving plane at fairly close range, fifty to one hundred feet. The maneuver was repeated for the next twelve or fourteen minutes. While we were coming down at the men, they would lie on the ground; when we moved off, they would get up and run. We would come down again, dive at them, and fire the rifle. Finally he pulled off, without hitting them, and I asked, "Does this happen often?" "All the time," he said. "Do you ever hit anyone in this way?" I asked, and he replied, "Not very often. It's hard to hit anybody from a plane with an M16, but it scares the shit out of them. They will be pretty scared VC tonight."

I asked him how he knew they were VC, and he answered, "There's nothing but VC in the Plain of Reeds." The Plain of Reeds was a free-fire zone, which meant we had condemned to death all those who might be found in it. I was later told that there were almost two thousand fishermen in the area who continued to fish during our attacks.

This game, this hunt, is something that goes on daily in almost every province of Vietnam. I am sure the Vietcong will come out of this war with great pride in the fact that they confronted American machines and survived. I came out of that plane ride with a strong sense of unease.

JAMES ARMSTRONG: The changing nature of the war in Vietnam has produced certain tragic cultural consequences that cannot be ignored. Congressman Conyers and I were privileged to serve on an eight-member study team in South Vietnam in the summer of 1969. We talked with government officials, members of the United States mission, President Nguyen Van Thieu, Prime Minister Tran Thien Khiem, Communists or alleged Vietcong agents in prisons. But we spent most of our time with members of the "third force."

We talked with Thich Tri Quang, who is considered the head of the militant Buddhists. Though he is a vigorous spokesman for a point of view, it would seem that he reflects the feelings of the majority of persons south of the Seventeenth Parallel. When we asked him to differentiate between French influence in Vietnam before our coming and present American influence, he said, "The French respected our traditions." The war that is being waged in Vietnam now is virtually destroying these traditions.

The countryside has been ravaged by defoliation measures and continuous fighting. This has driven the villagers from their homes, their hamlets, their family graveyards, either to the urban centers, where they join a glut of anonymous refugees, or to planned "refugee camps." The village, the hamlet, the family graveyard are all important, but they have been snatched from the people.

A second comment of Thich Tri Quang was, "Fortunately for us the French were poorer than you are." Not only our overwhelming technology but our tremendous fiscal presence has upturned the value system of Vietnam. The bar girl and the shoeshine boy can earn as much money as the head of a family or a member of the cabinet.

A culture has simply been turned around.

This, I think, we must understand: We say we are there to defend the Vietnamese civilian, yet of all the persons involved he is undoubtedly the primary casualty, the primary victim of the war.

REP. JOHN CONYERS, JR.: When I questioned American officials in Vietnam about the violence and oppression perpetrated against the Vietnamese by their own government, I received this kind of response: "Well, you know, we are dealing with Orientals now. They are not used to the same level of legality of conduct that we are. You cannot expect the prisons, the interrogation camps, the detention centers, the inquisitional methods and techniques that might be employed, to be comparable to ours. These are Orientals. You can't expect them to hold to what a white western society would regard as normal standards under these circumstances."

The attitude reflected in that comment raises the question of racism. Is not the racism inherent in this country relevant to some of our conduct toward the enemy in Vietnam? If the enemy were white, would we not treat him a bit differently?

JONATHAN SCHELL: I think the question of racism does arise, although it is hard to judge because we have no way of telling whether we would behave in a similar fashion toward a white enemy. But just the words used to describe the enemy in Vietnam—such as "gooks" and "slopes," meaning sloping eyes—certainly do indicate a strong element of racism in our soldiers' attitude toward the Vietnamese.

You see more of the Confederate flag in Vietnam than you see of the Stars and Stripes. You hear the kind of comment cited by Congressman Conyers that they have an "Oriental mentality." This is brought up again and again.

One man said to me, "You see, we have to torture them because they are two thousand years behind us, and the only thing they understand is force." The notion that the Vietnamese belong to a different, strange race, that they don't have the same kind of values we have, is certainly a very strong element in the way we have chosen to treat them.

GABRIEL KOLKO: The application of American power overseas is the one area in which the United States believes in equal rights.

The firebomb raids against Germany, which were carried on with the same kind of brutality in World War II, did not discriminate in favor of the white people of Germany. After the war, the first United States intervention overseas was against Greece, and it was carried on in a very bloody way, in an area that was exclusively white.

The United States planned its initial interventions after World War II essentially in Europe. It did, indeed, contemplate intervention in France, and drew up plans for that eventuality. I don't think the United States is fighting any differently in Vietnam than it would in France or in Spain, if that should prove necessary.

RICHARD FALK: I think it is significant that in the indictment of Lieutenant William L. Calley for his part in the massacre at My Lai the formal charge was that he participated in the murder of "Oriental human beings." That kind of language could not have survived all of the bureaucratic processes of review in any but a racist society.

In Vietnam we are dealing with both an alien culture, for which we have no sympathy or understanding, and a race we are able to dehumanize as part of the process of dissociating our consciences from the acts we are committing.

The situation is not comparable, I think, to World War II, in which our cruelty was basically carried out in fairly impersonal contexts. The Dresden raid and the firebombing do represent terrible acts of war, but they do not have the same kind of immediacy involved in the kind of warfare in which we are engaging in Vietnam.

GORDON LIVINGSTON: The analogy is depressingly clear between our failure to relate successfully to the Vietnamese and to the black people who comprise an "underdeveloped nation" within our own society. In both cases our behavior is racist in the true sense of opposing the overwhelming forces generated by a people's search for pride and identity.

At an operational level, most Americans simply do not care about the Vietnamese. In spite of our national protestations about self-determination, revolutionary development, and the like, the attitude of our people on the ground, military and civilian, is one of nearly universal contempt.

This arrogant feeling is manifested in a variety of ways, from indiscriminate destruction of lives and property to the demeaning handouts that pass for civic action. The Vietnamese, a sensitive and intelligent people, are well aware of our general lack of regard and generally reward our efforts with the indifference or hostility that they deserve. We in turn attempt to create the illusion of progress by generating meaningless statistics to support predictions of success which have proved invariably incorrect. And the dying goes on.

Specific examples of our disregard for the Vietnamese are legion. At one point the corps commander issued a document entitled "U.S.-Vietnamese Relations" detailing many of these instances. It represented official acknowledgement of the problem, but its exhortation to "avoid creating embarrassing incidents" was an exercise in futility. Numerous examples are available from my own experience, including the running down and killing of two Vietnamese women on bicycles with a *helicopter* (the pilot was exonerated); driving tracked vehicles through rice paddies; throwing C-ration cans at children from moving vehicles; running truck convoys through villages at high speed on dirt roads (if people are eating rice at the time it has to be thrown away because of the dust).

In the area of medical civic action, it was the policy to give no more than a two-day supply of medicine to any patient lest the excess fall into Vietcong hands. Since visits to any given village are generally infrequent, this meant that the illusion of medical care was just that.

Another example of the dehumanization of our relationships with the Vietnamese is evident when a civilian is admitted to one of our military hospitals. He is given a new name. In place of a perfectly adequate, pronounceable Vietnamese name, he is given an appellation that is easier for Americans to remember. The nature of some of the designations chosen reveals their impact and intent— "Bubbles," "Ohio," and "Cyclops" for a soldier who had lost an eye.

Finally, one need only listen to a conversation between Americans concerning Vietnamese to appreciate the general lack of regard. The universal designation for the people of Vietnam, friend or enemy, is "gook" (also "slope" and "dink"). On the whole, this has no conscious pejorative connotation as used casually, but it does say something about our underlying attitude toward those for whose sake we are ostensibly fighting. How we can presume to influence a struggle for the political loyalties of a people for whom we manifest such uniform disdain is to me the great unanswered, indeed unanswerable, question of this war.

HANS MORGENTHAU: I think it is uncontestable that the Vietnam war reflects the fact that we are fighting and killing a nonwhite race. After all, we did not collect the ears of German soldiers in World War II as mementos of our killing, but we have done so at a considerable scale in Vietnam.

JOHN B. SHEERIN: I am inclined to agree with Professor Kolko that the United States is racially impartial in its military destructiveness. It is also interesting to note that the South Vietnamese fighting for the Thieu regime are quite as savage and brutal toward the Vietcong or the North Vietnamese as are the Americans. In fact, we can safely say that they are quite as destructive as we are, except to the extent that they are inhibited by the lack of our technological potential for destructiveness.

ROBERT JAY LIFTON: There is a way in which the positions taken by Dr. Kolko and a number of others come together. It isn't exactly either-or; there are two disturbances in American policy. One is a matter of application of technology and force, especially toward revolutionary movements in the non-Western world, and the other is a matter of racism. Both of these can readily enhance any tendency toward psychic numbing and brutalization.

GABRIEL KOLKO: Let me state this a different way: The racism that the United States expresses in Vietnam is a manifestation of the fact that the United States is a racist society. But I do not think American racism is a major or causal element in the determination of U.S. foreign policy, and especially military policy.

The most important proof of this is that for more than twenty years American power required, cultivated, and built a strategic weapons system designed exclusively to do away with a white society—the Soviet Union. On this issue, the United States is very flexible.

GORDON LIVINGSTON: Responsibility for American actions in Vietnam cannot reasonably be ascribed to any small number of our representatives there, nor can it be attributed to some fundamental defect in human nature or the nature of war itself.

Our search for culprits leads us to the mirror of reality, there to confront ourselves with Walt Kelly's triumphant cry, "We have met the enemy and they is us."

America's presence in Vietnam, indeed its place in the world, is predicated on a self-image of moral rectitude. The belief in the essential humaneness and good will of Americans, even in time of war, is ingrained in our national mythology. The events in our history which contradict the myth are neither widely known nor celebrated, but they are there. For example, in the "incident" at My Lai some observers heard echoes of another day in 1890 when at Wounded Knee Creek, South Dakota, soldiers of the U.S. 7th Cavalry massacred about three hundred Sioux, most of them women and children, in what was the last significant event in the ignoble conquest of the American Indian.

The ethic of the legitimate use of violence is deeply rooted in our culture. Our folk heroes, real and imaginary, have almost all been violent men. The level of violence in our entertainment parallels that in our streets, and we have learned to accept, if not enjoy, both. The reporting of the war itself, with the incessant repetition of violent images, seems to produce, if I may borrow a term, psychic numbing on a national scale.

Dr. Maccoby made a profound and important observation when he described the war as the triumph of the principles and values of the industrial bureaucracy. In trying to describe the feeling I had toward the military organization of which I was a part in Vietnam, I have called it the "General Motors of Death." The magnitude of the effort, the paperwork, and the middle-management attitude of many of the participants, as well as the predilection for charts and statistics—including that most dehumanizing and absurd figure of all, the body count— all these represent the triumph of technocracy over rea- son. One has the distinct impression that a majority of Americans object to this war not because it is wrong, but because it is so demonstrably inefficient.

Nevertheless, we think of ourselves as a peace-loving people, slow to anger, quick to forgive. The ideals for which we have fought our wars have been clearly stated and almost universally supported. More than this, the manner in which we prosecuted the fighting has been accepted as reflecting a moral superiority over our ene- mies which has found expression in the sanctimonious and chauvinistic assumption of "God on our side." Implicit in this view of our country reluctantly at war was a picture of the American soldier as a character out of a Mauldin cartoon—a flower in his helmet, a candy bar in his hand for the children of the war, determinedly but decently fighting to roll back the well-identified forces which were the current threat to human freedom.

What, then, happened at My Lai? What does it say about us as a people and about the war we have chosen to wage in Vietnam? To answer this, we might try to consider the total impact of our presence there, with spe- cial emphasis on relations between Americans and the people of Vietnam, for herein lies the key to the tragedy that is war.

In addition to the bombs and the napalm, we have ex- ported to Vietnam some of the most degrading aspects of American culture. For example, drug use among the U.S. troops is so widespread as to have reached epidemic pro- portions. The magnitude of the problem is impossible to document accurately, but estimates of drug experimenta- tion run as high as 80 per cent of the troops, with many of them becoming habituated. The boredom, loneliness, and anxiety engendered by their situation make many soldiers welcome this form of escape. Vietnam, unlike some other Oriental nations, does not have a tradition of widespread narcotic usage, but there have been some changes since we arrived. The American market has been exploited by Vietnamese entrepreneurs whose own society did not generate sufficient demand to support them before we came.

Among the basic services which the Vietnamese economy provides our forces is prostitution. Venereal disease is, in fact, consistently the health problem of highest incidence among U.S. troops. Even in relatively remote rural areas our units are magnets for the aptly named "short-time girls." Often they are brought from a distance and are received by the local Vietnamese with the same lack of enthusiasm one would find in a small town in this country in an equivalent situation.

A related and particularly tragic aspect of our presence in Vietnam—and perhaps the one with the most lasting consequences—is in the large number of children of mixed parentage who have been produced and abandoned there. Pearl Buck has coined the term "Amerasian children," but by whatever name their abandonment represents the ultimate in our contemptuous treatment of that people. At some of the orphanages fully half the infants are of American fathers. They lie there, bottles propped against their bassinets, facing a future of rejection in an ethnically proud society. Perhaps someone could include them in a separate body count.

Even our best impulses founder for lack of understanding or caring. For example, there is the Medical Civic Action Program (MEDCAP). The concept is simple enough: Medical personnel go out to a local village, set up shop, and provide treatment for whomever needs it. The Vietnamese, of course, respond enthusiastically to this opportunity to receive the benefits of modern medical science and flock to be treated. Unfortunately, treatment is limited by several circumstances.

First, diagnosis is complicated by the difficulty of getting symptoms through an interpreter; diagnostic tools available include the stethoscope and the doctor's clinical acumen. More important, however, is the complete inability adequately to treat any but the most superficial problems. Any given village is unlikely to be visited more often than every two months, if that, and official policy is to restrict distribution of medicines to a two-day supply lest excess fall to the Vietcong. Facilities are not generally available for evacuation of those cases needing hospitalization. The result of all this is a parody of medical care unsatisfying either to patients or physicians, most of the latter of whom feel quite cynical about their role in this charade. One cannot long treat obvious cases of tuberculosis with cough medicine and still retain a feeling of professional competence. Such a purely symbolic exercise, however, produces multitudes of pictures for home consumption of Americans looking concerned about Vietnamese; it also generates some of those statistics which are the indices of "progress" cited by those who decide how much dying it takes till we finally reach that light at the end of the tunnel.

The medical evacuation helicopter pilots in Vietnam are widely respected for their willingness to fly extremely dangerous missions to evacuate wounded. When a life is at stake, they will spare no risk—as long as it is an American life. Two incidents demonstrate this vividly. I spent a night in a village in I Corps in which six Vietnamese women were wounded by a grenade. I felt it doubtful that one of them would survive without prompt evacuation and so stated in my radioed request for a helicopter. The request was refused, although, based on my experience in circumstances of similar risk, I was convinced the mission would have been flown for a wounded American.

The second incident involved a nineteen-year-old U.S. soldier, a chaplain's assistant, who was shot one night in a village adjacent to a U.S. encampment. The radio message was mistransmitted so that the helicopter pilot understood the wounded to be a Vietcong. He declined to come into a landing zone close to the wounded man, and while the soldier was being transported overland to a safer area he died—a case, one might say, of mistaken identity.

It is not difficult to document the magnitude of the American contempt for the Vietnamese. The images of my own experience abound: the riddled body of a Vietcong soldier dumped from an American armored vehicle before a crowd in his native village which included his family; the bloody results of a collision on a narrow road of an eight-passenger tri-Lambretta with a speeding American five-ton truck; the spectacle of a pilot forcing a Vietnamese to dive from his sampan to avoid being hit with helicopter skids; or a nurse in an American hospital who announced as "just another gook" a young boy with a shattered leg on whom an American orthopedic surgeon declined to operate, sending the boy instead to the province hospital where the leg was surely amputated.

The situation is only slightly mitigated by the presence in Vietnam of those Americans who *do* care about the people there. There are physicians who routinely and without pretension give of themselves and their time to provide effective medical care. There are soldiers at all levels who try in any way they can to express warmth for Vietnamese. Some even pay them the ultimate compliment of learning a bit of their language (though it should be noted that it is a more common form of cultural exchange to set up English classes for the Vietnamese). Many of the civilian agencies there give freely of American expertise in agriculture, education, and health in a way that promotes Vietnamese participation. This is not to state, however, that there is a balance struck between our good works and our destructive efforts. There is no comparison, either in expenditure of effort or accomplishment of purpose.

And then there are the "atrocities." It is clear that My Lai was remarkable only for the magnitude of the slaughter; individual acts of brutality are a daily fact of this war as they have been in all wars. They can be either planned or indiscriminate, the distinction being decidedly academic to the victims. What is special about Vietnam is the widespread pretense that such acts are not systematically occurring. Mistreatment of prisoners, for example, takes many forms. Unlike American casualties, who are taken directly by helicopter to large hospitals with full surgical facilities, it is the practice to interrogate wounded Vietcong and North Vietnamese soldiers before evacuation. While providing first aid for one badly hit Vietcong, I was told by a senior officer, "We just need to keep him alive for a few minutes so we can question him. After that he can die; it doesn't matter to me." On another occasion an intelligence officer objected to my giving morphine to a wounded prisoner, saying, "I think they talk better when they're in a little pain." South Vietnamese National Police working on American operations tortured prisoners routinely. Beatings or the water torture (pouring water on a cloth held over the mouth and nose) provide field expedients, while at district and province headquarters more sophisticated techniques include the use of hand-crank telephones to apply electric shocks to various parts of the body. This was characterized to me by one American adviser as the "Bell Telephone Hour."

At a time when my unit was considering the use of sodium pentothal in interrogations, one senior anesthesiologist, a Medical Corps lieutenant colonel, offered to administer succinyl choline to prisoners to provide temporary paralysis of the muscles of respiration. Although the suggestion was not acted on in this case, reports were current of its use elsewhere.

The indiscriminate killing of civilians, particularly in free-fire zones, is by now such an accepted fact of the war that it seems a cliché to mention it. But this acceptance is at once our shame and the warrant for more.

The final atrocity has been dealt the land itself, an area about the size of Florida marked now by three million craters which, for hundreds of square miles, make the country we would defend resemble in grotesque mimicry that other great American objective—the moon.

The shock and self-accusation expressed (even reveled in) in many quarters of this country at the My Lai disclosures have been often notable for a failure to perceive the continuity of indifference and brutality of which this event forms only a part. It is as if our tolerance for immorality was quantitative, as if murder by the hundreds was necessary to compel our interest. This concept has some relevance when the President enlists support for a policy of gradual withdrawal by reducing casualties (American, of course) in the belief, seemingly justified, that there is a level of death which the people of this country will tolerate. If this is so, then we shall have indeed forfeited our allegiance to the ideals of individual worth and human dignity on which this republic was founded. And those whom we would victimize will not be long foreclosing the judgment of history upon us—as they have already done in Vietnam.

I should like to close with an account of my Christmas Eve in 1968. I was sitting down to supper at the 7th Surgical Hospital in II Corps when the medical evacuation helicopters began arriving. Their cargo was children. Over the radio one of the pilots was heard to report, "Jesus, they're glowing in the dark." In the next twenty minutes we received thirty-three youngsters and one adult burned to varying degrees by white phosphorus. They came in two and three to a stretcher. Several were blinded. All were still burning. Five died that night. The remainder will carry the scars all the days of their lives.

The adult had apparently set off the explosion in the crowd of children, thinking it was a smoke grenade. Like so much of the misery, intentional and accidental, in Vietnam, that grenade was made in the U.S.A. Children everywhere comprise mankind's unrepresented constituency. They do not deserve to be dead or blinded, two to a stretcher, in a world of our creation.

FRANK KOWALSKI: Each of us has brought to this discussion views and ideas conditioned by his background and experiences. Though I have served in Congress and have tasted both the sweet and bitter of politics, I spent most of my adult life in the Army. Accordingly, I would like to comment essentially from that background.

To begin with, soldiers don't make wars—they die in them. We are not in the senseless war in Vietnam because any mad-dog general or militarists decided to wage war there. We backed into that bottomless pit through a series of mistakes and misguided policies of a succession of Presidents—with the acquiescence of Congress.

Nor can we put the blame for the way the war is fought in Vietnam on the military. The Army, Navy, and Air Force have a fantastic assortment of horrendous weapons available not only to destroy North Vietnam but to wipe civilization from this planet. The weapons and strategies the military employ in Vietnam, however, are determined by the legally constituted heads of our civilian Government. We have not used nuclear and biological weapons there because the President of the United States has not authorized their use. On the other hand, we have carpet-bombed North Vietnam, blasted forests, jungles, rice paddies, towns, and villages in South Vietnam, spewed flaming napalm on both friend and foe, defoliated hundreds of square miles of Asia, herded millions of people about the country like cattle, and crushed and made governments at will, because the Presidents of the United States, past and present, either initiated or approved the use of these strategies of war in that unhappy land. Specifically, there is no evidence that the military of the United States violated any instructions of the Administration in power regarding limitations on the use of weapons or the strategies to be employed.

There is evidence, however—distressing evidence—that a deplorable slippage in behavior has been developing in the military structure. In Vietnam this slippage is the natural consequence of fighting a war we cannot win. The resulting frustration unhinges men at all levels from traditional American concern for humanity. In a war where the enemy is everywhere and nowhere at the same time, military men no longer plan or hope for victory—they seek only to survive themselves and to punish the "gooks." And so, if designated targets cannot be bombed, bomb loads are dumped on anything that moves or on any area that looks like enemy ground. When one cannot come to grips with the enemy on the battle field, assassination of suspected "gooks" becomes acceptable to men who otherwise abhor murder. Prisoners and civilians are shot on orders or on a whim, dragged behind trucks, dumped into the sea, or thrown out of aircraft. When the elusive guerrillas fade into the jungle, frustrated troops get some consolation in venting their artillery, mortars, or rockets on a village through which the enemy escaped. The massacre at My Lai, accordingly, where not even babies were spared, was the inevitable consequence of a gradual erosion of human restraints and military controls. I want to believe that this monstrous slippage in conscience has infected individuals rather than the body of our military.

In light of my long service in the Army, I am convinced that there are sincere military men who deplore, as much as I do, the wholesale dishonor My Lai has heaped upon American men and units fighting in Vietnam. Moreover, I am sure these men are doing everything in their power to cleanse the Army from within.

Specifically, I applaud the Army for bringing to trial the

officers and men who participated in the My Lai and other killings of civilians and prisoners in Vietnam. Whatever may be the outcome of these courts-martial—and certainly those charged must be assumed innocent until found guilty by proper authorities—the Army command, by initiating these trials, has served notice on its young officers and men, those engaged in close combat, that the military will not tolerate wanton killings. In this action the Army is responding to the spirit of Nuremberg and the conscience of humanity.

Secondly, the Peers Panel, constituted by the Army to investigate the behavior of higher echelons of command in the My Lai incident, is a clear effort by the military to fix responsibility of senior officers for the actions of their men and units towards civilians in war. If this indeed proves to be the purpose of the Peers Panel, the Army deserves the most considerate encouragement. It also warrants our closest attention. I would urge Members of Congress to take necessary steps at the appropriate time to ensure that the Department of Defense releases to the public a full report of the panel's findings and recommendations for widest possible discussion. Only through a thorough and critical examination by the public of the behavior and responsibilities of our senior commanders in the My Lai action can America hope to avoid future dishonors in war.

Finally, I think the Department of Defense should be urged to take two specific actions:

1. The Secretary of Defense should appoint a commission of distinguished military and civilian jurists to examine our military code of justice with a view to making such changes as may be appropriate to ensure that American traditions of moral behavior in war, as well as the spirit of Nuremberg, are fully incorporated in that code.

2. The Secretary of Defense should direct the services to incorporate in their school systems—from the military academies through the National War College—and in

their various training program, courses of instruction designed to indoctrinate men and officers at all levels regarding their human responsibilities as soldiers of a great democracy and the overriding obligations of command towards civilian populations in war.

GORDON LIVINGSTON: We are developing much too narrow a view of what can be done. It is easy to make the military the whipping boy and say there has been a deficit in training, for example, for the average American soldier. But in fact what we are saying is the same thing Mrs. Meadlo said to CBS after her son admitted he had killed thirty-five or forty men, women, and children at My Lai: "I sent them a good boy and they made him a murderer." In fact, she hadn't sent them a good boy. The boys who go into the military are all capable of doing that sort of thing.

I am speaking from some direct experience. I have participated as an observer on search-and-destroy missions. I have flown gun missions over free-fire zones, and I can assure you that there is not only a disregard for Vietnamese life, there is complete brutalization. There is nothing that is not fired at in those free-fire zones, including animals and birds. If you can imagine shooting at a deer with a weapon that fires 5,000 rounds a minute, I think you can understand the absurdity of the idea that somehow we can train people to show a bit more consideration.

From the time an American steps off an airplane there and sees the people of Vietnam, hears them referred to as "gooks," and begins to refer to them as "gooks" himself, he has taken the step that is necessary to participate in something like My Lai. The answer does not lie in better training programs for the military. We must accuse ourselves and our society. We are not going to get away with anything less fundamental than that.

IV

INDIVIDUAL CONSCIENCE:

The Moral Challenge

"We should pay tribute to that small but courageous number of the American armed forces who have refused over the years to follow orders when it came to the indiscriminate killing of civilians. . . . These are heroes whom we ought to remember and honor—not only for their own sake, but because they provide us with an example of what individual conscience can do against the immorality of an act of Government."

—HANS MORGENTHAU

JAMES ARMSTRONG: On March 16, 1968, Company C landed at a village called My Lai in South Vietnam under orders to "destroy it and all its inhabitants." Private First Class Michael Bernhardt, a textbook soldier in almost every respect—trained by Green Berets in his Miami R.O.T.C. days, a student at LaSalle Military Academy before that—kept his rifle slung on his shoulder with its muzzle pointed to the ground. He refused to shoot old men and women and children. He refused to follow orders. Paul David Meadlo, on the other hand, followed orders. His mother says, "I sent them a good boy and they made him a murderer." The question: What is a soldier's responsibility—or, for that matter, a citizen's responsibility—when his conscience comes into conflict with the laws of the state or the orders of governmental authority? The issue is not clear.

Socrates, standing before an Athenian tribunal, said, "I shall obey God rather than you. . . . Either acquit me or not; but whichever you do, understand that I will never alter my ways, not even if I have to die many times." But, according to Plato, a month later in his death cell the same man said, "A man must do what his city and his country order him." Justice Abe Fortas, of much later vintage, doesn't help much. He wrote: "If I had lived in Germany (under Hitler) or had been a Negro living in Birmingham . . . I hope I would have refused to wear an armband, to *Heil Hitler*, to submit to genocide . . . I hope I would have disobeyed the state law that said I might not enter the waiting room reserved for 'whites.' " He goes on to say, however, that he would never condone "efforts to overthrow the Government or to seize control of an area or parts of it by force," without explaining how there could be a mass protest against Nazi or racist oppression without the probability of "force," of violence.

The conflict is an obvious one. Is the individual conscience of man ever justified in challenging and defying the collective conscience of the state? In a sense the conflict pits legal structures, political realities, and social "stability" against the individual's sense of dignity, worth, "rightness," and personal responsibility.

Conceivably the state can epitomize bestiality, as it did in Nazi Germany. Its laws and customs can violate the free spirit of man, as in a military government, a Communist police state, a racist nation or region, a segregated school district or suburban housing development. Make no mistake about it: Historically, governments have betrayed "the common good" time and time again. *We can expect even the most enlightened state to protect its interests and preserve its structures by denying its citizens certain liberties.* To suggest that there is absolute individual freedom in the United States is transparently untrue. What of compulsory education, taxation, military conscription, and laws that dictate whom a man will serve and sell to? What about a President who was not elected by a majority of the people, a costly, tragic war that has never been declared, our country's contribution to the international anarchy that makes each nation a law unto itself, and the possibilities of a push-button holocaust that could destroy us all without our individual knowledge or consent? And at a more subtle level of public policy, what about a man like Representative Mendel Rivers, functioning behind closed doors, exercising unbelievable influence over defense budgets, national priorities, and the militarization of a nation—without *my* consent, without *your* consent?

There is no way for any man to be totally free. The individual's life is always conditioned by time, place, and circumstance. He can never extract himself from his cultural and political context. But, granting the "givens" of his existence, what recourse has he to challenge the establishments of his world; to protest, to dissent, to declare his independence as his forefathers did? Well, he can throw the tea into Boston Harbor; he can try to take Bunker Hill. Or, if he doesn't feel impelled to go that far, he can follow the example of certain Quaker judges in colonial Pennsylvania (or, more recently, Charles Lindbergh in his government's "defense" program) and simply withdraw from structured public responsibility rather than engage in procedures and policies his conscience rebels against. He can refuse to fire his gun, as Private Bernhardt at My Lai did; or resist the draft; or face court-martial proceedings because of his opposition to the Vietnam war, as Captain Howard Levy did; or burn himself to death like a Buddhist monk; or, far this side of such a melodramatic gesture, he can simply insist on doing his own thing in his own way.

The free man will not look to the state to "give" him his freedom. He will claim it, affirm it, make his decisions on the basis of it, and *willingly accept the consequences.* The man who functions on the basis of only those rights and liberties guaranteed by the state (whether he lives in Hanoi, Moscow, Peking, Saigon, or Kalamazoo) is not free. He has permitted the state to define the limits of his selfhood.

The free and responsible man will support and refine man-made laws wherever possible, but he will not permit his conscience to be limited by statute or its application. If he is a religious man, he will appeal to transcendent authority and join St. Peter in saying, "We must obey God rather than man." He will "seek first" God's kingdom, insisting that every other loyalty is a lesser loyalty. Or, lacking the authority of revelation, he may join Thoreau in refusing to pay taxes, in denouncing legalized racism and an unjust war, appealing to the "general right and obligation of men to disobey commands of a government" which they consider morally wrong.

Flag-waving chauvinism must be recognized for exactly what it is. If Auschwitz was inhumane, so was Hiroshima. If the murder of kulaks was wrong in Stalin's Russia, so was the relocation of Nisei Americans during World War II. Vietcong terrorism is harsh reality. The Hue massacre *happened* during the Tet offensive of 1968. But Vietcong terrorism does not justify the My Lai massacre or the murder of Thai Khac Chuyen by the Green Berets— Chuyen's widow cried, "I thought they were saving us from the Vietcong, but I see now that they are just as bad as the Vietcong"—nor does it justify General Thieu's kan-

garoo courts, the "military field courts" of the Saigon government. *Atrocities are not legitimatized by being Ameri-
canized.* William Lloyd Garrison said it far better than I:
"Our country is the world, our countrymen are all mankind. . . . The interests, rights, liberties of American citizens are no more dear to us, than those of the whole
human race."

Today *our* nation is involved in an immoral war in
Southeast Asia. It is spending $70 billion a year on a war
economy, permitting a military-industrial complex to
dominate national policy with no effective system of
checks and balances. And while the Pentagon grows more
truculent and the Administration consciously escalates
the arms race with its missile and antimissile talk, the Vice
President of the United States scattershots his purple in-
vective, badgering the finest newspapers and the most
responsible television commentators in the land, branding
conscientious citizens "political hustlers," "merchants of
hate," and "ideological eunuchs," and lashing out at what
he calls the "whole damn zoo" of youthful dissenters. It
can happen here. It might well be *happening* here. Our
nation is not the near-Utopia envisioned by our forefathers. There is an essential place in this and every state for
a Martin Luther King to write from his Birmingham jail:
"I think we have moral obligations to obey just laws. On
the other hand, I think we have moral obligations to disobey unjust laws because non-cooperation with evil is just
as much a moral obligation as cooperation with good." The
lessons of the Third Reich may have slipped from our
memories much too soon.

I am not an anarchist. I would, however, appeal to the
Hegelian dialectic. If the thesis is the will of the state and
the antithesis is the conscience of the individual, then I
must come down firmly on the side of individual conscience. Only if individual liberties are stressed will the

emerging synthesis reinforce the structures of freedom. The state has everything going for it—the military, the courts, unprecedented fiscal and political power, the entire sprawling apparatus of government. *In this kind of world, the individual must be encouraged to be true to himself;* this is the highest possible patriotism.

Henry Thoreau was once scheduled to deliver an address called "A Plea for Captain John Brown." Sensing and reflecting the mood of the community, the sexton refused to ring the bell announcing the meeting, whereupon Thoreau rang it himself. That is the acceptance of individual responsibility. There are bells to be rung, rights to be championed, causes to be served, and if we allow individual conscience to be swallowed up in the will of an impersonal state, then there will literally be hell to pay.

HANS MORGENTHAU: We should pay tribute to that small but courageous number of members of the American armed forces who have refused over the years to follow orders when it came to the indiscriminate killing of civilians.

A magazine called *Flying*, which I don't read regularly, published a report on our operations in the air over Vietnam and cited a number of instances in which bombs were deliberately dropped on vacant fields or naval fire was deliberately directed away from civilian villages. The servicemen who did this were either court-martialed or declared insane—because, after all, it is insane not to participate in an insane operation in which everyone else takes part.

These are heroes whom we ought to remember and honor—not only for their own sake, but because they provide us with an example of what individual conscience can do against the immorality of an act of Government.

It seems to me that at this stage of the public debate on Vietnam, the main emphasis ought to be put not upon the

delusions which led to the war, not upon its political aim-
lessness or military absurdity, but upon the moral aspects
that have come to the fore because of the massacre at My
Lai. One has to insist upon the moral inacceptability of
this kind of war.

Everything else—every pragmatical consideration—
ought to yield to this fundamental moral refusal to support
such a war.

WILLIAM P. THOMPSON: Both the Nuremberg and Tokyo
courts enforced the doctrine that the individual is obli-
gated, in some circumstances, to violate the orders and
the established policies of government. Similarly, the
church has taught that when there is a conflict between
loyalty to God and loyalty to the state, loyalty to God must
prevail.

But this formulation confronts us with a very trou-
blesome dilemma. On the one hand we espouse the principle of a higher loyalty, whether to God or to some sense
of humanity; on the other hand we enact laws that make
it criminal to follow that higher law. It seems to me that
at the very least we have an obligation to reverse our laws
so that they recognize those obligations which we imposed upon our defeated enemies after World War II.

We ought also to acknowledge in law the principle of
the just war that some religions have taught, which gives
an individual the right to refuse to participate in a war he
finds unjust. In other words, our Selective Service laws
should be amended to incorporate the principle of selective conscientious objection. If we fail to do this simple
thing, it seems to me, our churches and citizens of good
will will need to find ways of supporting a whole new
generation of martyrs.

JOHN B. SHEERIN: It has been suggested that we are paying too much attention to the trial and punishment of
individuals involved in specific atrocities—that we should

concentrate, instead, on trying to prevent this sort of thing from happening. But it seems to me that the quickest and perhaps most effective way to get at the fundamental causes is through the persons of individual defendants. I do not believe that the press and television should be curbed in presenting the news about individuals involved in war crimes trials. Through a dramatization of individual guilt, we can get down to the more important questions, the hard questions of collective guilt.

This is the theme of many of our young people—that there is not only the guilt of individual persons, but also the evil in our social structure. Whether you call it guilt or evil does not matter very much: It is there, in the structures of our society and especially in the structure of the military establishment. And it seems to me that the best way to reveal it is through those individuals who symbolize and dramatize the more abstract and impersonal evil in society.

STEWART MEACHAM: The basic problem, it seems to me, is not that laws are being broken—though this, of course, is bad and should be corrected. But I sense that the Vietnam war is doing something even worse; it is destroying the basic commitments on which the very concepts of legality and legitimacy rest. This strikes at our fundamental capacity to survive as a society. A very large percentage of our population, indeed possibly every one of us in one way or another, is being forced into a position that makes legitimacy impossible.

I don't see how we can build a society that has valid concepts of legitimacy when so many Americans are expending so much energy and money in practices that are illegitimate and morally indefensible. I am talking about those who make and execute our policies, but I am also talking about the factory worker who spends his days making one small part that happens to be a component of a terror weapon which is, in turn, a component of our complex, atrocious, and criminal war machine.

There are other victims. There are GIs actually engaged in criminal tactics. And there are our own young people here at home. When Abbie Hoffman was identifying himself in the Chicago conspiracy trial, he said he was a member of the Woodstock nation, and this seemed amusing to some people and impertinent to others; but there were many young people in this country who knew what he was talking about. They are the stateless people in our very midst who are responding, as best they can, to the basic illegitimacy dramatized by our war crimes in Vietnam.

I think we are moving into a constitutional crisis because the Executive Branch, the Congress, and the courts have failed to come to grips with these issues. Many in the peace movement now feel that the only thing left to them in the constitutional context is freedom of speech and assembly, and many are wondering now if these are not the next areas to be denied.

The most hopeful sign is that we are not yet afraid, as we were during the Joe McCarthy period.

We need to talk in meaningful ways about war crimes and violence. We need to find some common denominator of decency in action that we can all accept. Perhaps, out of such thought and discussion of what we must do in churches, in universities, in trade unions, with young people, with men in the armed forces, with people in the peace movement, we may discover a way to remain together—a way that, even at this late hour, can produce a program of action and basic change.

DANIEL ELLSBERG: Who is it that we're talking to? Who is it that we want to hear us? Whose behavior would we like to change? We have raised questions of obedience and responsibility—whose sense of these matters would we like most to affect? Could it be that of soldiers in the field, in the chaos of battle, whose moral choices are made under enormous pressures and under fear of death? This is a worthwhile aim, but it cannot be our main objective, I would think.

The attitudes and behavior I would most like to change are those of my former colleagues in the U.S. Government. I speak not as a researcher but from experience as a former official of the Defense Department and the State Department in Washington and Vietnam—experience that makes me a possible defendant in a future war crimes trial. Some ten years ago I read the transcript of the Nuremberg trials, and that left me with the sense of what an exhibit in a war crimes trial looks like. As I was working in the Department of Defense, I did in some cases have a feeling while reading documents late at night that I was looking at future exhibits. Indeed, if we are to believe published accounts of contingency plans that have been prepared, for example, for war in Central Europe (such as might arise over Berlin), there even exist in locked safes in Washington right now documents that could very aptly be described as plans for escalatory genocide.

Such alleged plans reflect decisions by civilian officials which, I suggest, should be subjected in the future to more conscientious review. It is unusual for officials to ask, as they draw up such plans: Are these prudent? Are these mistaken? But it is most unusual—almost unknown—for them to ask as well: Does the United States have a right to do such things? And if not, do these officials have a duty to participate or a duty to resist?

A way of causing such questions to be asked in the future is to recognize, protect, reward, and encourage those individuals who might indeed apply such judgments, discuss them with their colleagues, and act on them.

Notice that in the massacre at My Lai and in other such military incidents there were individuals who, despite apparent risk to their lives, did resist the atrocities or at least fail to cooperate. It is a terrible shame—one that I share as a former official—that I know of no civilian official in the Government who has acted comparably in any area of the Vietnam involvement.

Individual acts of initiative and courage cannot, of course, bear the burden of preventing catastrophes like Vietnam. Institutional and political changes are essential. Yet even if these changes do occur, I believe that we cannot avoid much, much worse crimes and horrors than we have seen in the past unless many individuals within the Government do assume greater risks and a greater sense of responsibility than has been shown in the past decade.

Congress should reduce its tolerance of secrecy by the Executive, if only to protect its own need to know the facts. It should act to protect the right of dissent in general and, above all, the right of newspapermen to comment and to report truthfully.

Finally, I would strongly endorse the suggestion that selective conscientious objection be recognized in the draft law. The absence of such legislation has resulted in the imprisonment of young people who have chosen to act more responsibly, more conscientiously, than any other Americans I know.

JEROME FRANK: The rules governing conduct differ drastically in times of peace and war. In peacetime, conduct of members of society toward each other is regulated by laws embodying certain generally accepted values concerning the proper balance between the rights of the individual and the needs of the society to which he belongs. Relations towards members of other groups are also governed by codes protecting the rights of each.

In war these safeguards are swept away. In the past, this change was conventionally signalized by a formal declaration of war which, in effect, officially proclaimed that one's own nation was engaged in a life-and-death struggle with another one. Since the survival of the group takes precedence over the lives of its members, once a state of war exists, individual members of a society are expected to submit completely to the demands of the group, even to the point of sacrificing their lives. At the same time, since enemies are threats to the group's survival, this abolishes all inhibitions against killing them which might otherwise apply to them as fellow members of the human race. The enemy is seen as bestial in that he commits subhuman atrocities, and demonic in that he personifies a world view antithetical to one's own. In this connection it is interestng that the word "enemy" is characteristically preceded by the definite article—*the* enemy, not *an* enemy or even *our* enemy—as if he is the enemy not only of ourselves, but of mankind.

As long as the outcome of war was decided by organized, uniformed armies, it was possible to mitigate the ferocity of this view of the enemy by restricting the infliction of violence to the opposing armed forces. At the same time, inhibitions against intraspecies slaughter that we share with all living creatures were embodied in "laws of war." That is, it was considered a war crime to wantonly attack members of the enemy whose fate was irrelevant to the outcome of the struggle—people who could not harm you and whose death could in no way contribute to your victory. These included children, women, the aged and infirm, and disarmed prisoners. In such circumstances it made sense to ask, for example, whether the assassination of a leader or the use of napalm against a civilian was or was not a war crime.

To be sure, the "laws of war" protecting noncombatants and the helpless have always been honored as much in the breach as in the observance, probably because even women and children partake of the enemy image and because, under the emotional stresses of suffering, deprivation, and desire for revenge, combat soldiers' inhibitions against aggression are weakened. Nevertheless, such acts have never been condoned, and their perpetrators have often been punished when caught.

Today a nation's war potential, however, no longer depends solely or even primarily on its army, but on its industrial capacity. As a result, all productive citizens become combatants. This has led to total war, in which by far the most massive and indiscriminate killing and torturing is not inflicted by armies on each other but by bombs and shells on civilians. Why this slaughter is not considered to be an atrocity and does not arouse the same revulsion as individual killing of civilians remains something of a psychological mystery. Partly it may be attributed to a failure of imagination. It is easy to visualize the death of an individual, but not of a thousand or a million. One is reminded of the agonized concern of many Americans a few years ago over the fate of a child who fell down a well, but their indifference to the simultaneous deaths of millions elsewhere in the world from starvation, disease, and massacres. Another relevant aspect may be that, not seeing the consequences of his actions, the bombardier can never be sure how many, if any, persons were killed or maimed by the bomb, whereas there is no escaping responsibility for the death of the person you have killed before your eyes.

In any case, as wars have become total and the distinction between combatants and noncombatants has become increasingly blurred, it has become almost impossible to maintain a distinction between legal and illegal acts of war. If the deaths of civilians contribute to the victory of your nation as much as the deaths of fighting men, then civilians are legitimate targets for aggression.

Just as the entire population of a nation assumes a combatant role in modern war, so at the personal level the distinctions between combatants and noncombatants can often no longer be maintained. The enemy soldier cannot be identified by his uniform; he may be dressed as a peasant. And the young child, crippled old man, or nursing mother may hurl a grenade at you or stab you in the back. So the bewildered, exhausted combat soldier, sleepless, hungry, frightened, and thirsting for revenge, is all too prone to attack a potential enemy first, whether it be a woman or child, and ask questions afterwards. Nor can it be denied that under some circumstances humans are motivated by a blood lust which is akin to sexual lust and which, like it, can lead to wild excesses.

To complicate the picture further, the distinction between states of war and of peace has become increasingly tenuous. Nations slip into bloody conflicts without declaring war on each other, and it may well be that declarations of war are obsolete. Furthermore, many wars are no longer fought by nations as units, but by countries ravaged by internal conflicts, in which warring internal factions are themselves supported by rival outside powers.

In short, whatever tidiness old-fashioned wars may have possessed has disappeared, and with it, attempts to define war crimes are doomed to futility. Under the anarchic conditions of modern war the aim of each side must be to destroy the other's will to resist by the most efficient means at its disposal, whether it be assassination, napalming, or formal combat. The ultimate crime is war itself, and trying to assign degrees of criminality to certain of its forms is like trying to disguise the stench of rotting carcass by pouring perfume on it.

There remains the difficult question of the effect on young men who perform acts which, even though carried out in the heat of battle and often under orders, violate the codes of conduct in which they have been reared. In every society, the killing of the apparently defenseless is viewed as murder, and the guilt for this act is not necessarily washed away by the fact that the victim was an enemy and might have killed you first.

To be sure, humans show a truly remarkable ingenuity in finding ways to reconcile contradictions between their behavior and their beliefs. Passing the buck to a superior is the chief way by which men exculpate themselves from the consequences of their acts. All organized society rests on a hierarchical system in which subordinates obey the orders of their superiors. The power of obedience in such situations is immense—in fact, societies could probably not exist without it. It has been shown that about two-thirds of normal American civilians will deliver an electric shock they believe to be severe, painful, and possibly lethal to an inoffensive stranger they have never seen before, if ordered to do so by a person they regard as possessing legitimate authority. It is as if the authority bears the responsibility, and their own conscience is thereby absolved. How much easier it is to obey an order to kill civilians, who may or may not be enemies, in the midst of a war.

So it seems probable that, by and large, returning combat soldiers will attribute their murderous acts to the circumstances of war, and will, with clear consciences, return to their roles as peaceful, law-abiding citizens when they doff their uniforms. At least, this has been generally true following past wars, although, to be sure, there has been a slight increase in violent crime on the part of the returning soldiers.

This optimistic conclusion must, however, be qualified by certain special conditions of the Vietnam war. The returning soldier's readiness to resume his former role in society depends on how fully he accepted the standards and values of the society that sent him to war in the first place. Many servicemen today do not accept the justifications for sending them to risk their lives in Vietnam, and some, in fact, may regard the real enemy as the "Establishment" rather than the North Vietnamese. They have seriously questioned the right of the power structure to command their allegiance.

The domestic situation is further complicated by the polarization of American society into conflicting groups who have come to see each other as enemies. These perceptions will be intensified by the search for scapegoats, by returning soldiers who, if they have not been defeated, certainly have not been victorious. In such cases the universal way for an army to preserve its self-esteem is to identify a group at home who, to use the phrase popular in Germany after World War I, delivered a "stab in the back" but accounted for their defeat. These rifts in our social and political fabric will be exacerbated by returning veterans, and how they can be countered should be a matter of utmost concern. If not, in the end, the chief loser in the Vietnam war may be the United States itself.

While the immediate future may be fraught with peril, two long-term trends hold out hopes that such disasters as the Vietnam war will not be repeated. The first is the growing sense of community among all the world's people, fostered by mass telecommunications, mass transportation, and now especially the views of the earth from the moon. We are rapidly coming to realize that we are all passengers on the same crowded spaceship who can only survive by devoting our full energies to combatting the dangers that threaten us all equally, regardless of nationality or race—overpopulation, war, and pollution of the biosphere. These may be the superordinate goals that will, before too late, divert us from our present self-destructive course. Finally, and along the same lines, the causes over which wars were fought in the past—resources, territory, population—are losing their justification. As the world moves into an economy of abundance, nations no longer will need each other's resources. At the same time, the effort to control hostile populations and territories is becoming ever more costly. Conquered territories and populations have become drains on national strength rather than contributors to it.

As tangible occasions for internation conflict diminish in importance, however, ideological causes assume increasing prominence. Today's wars resemble the religious wars of the past; that is, the conflict is not over control of territory or resources, but over whose view of the future shall prevail, or what form of social organization will contribute most to human happiness. If history teaches anything, it is that although these issues have been prolific causes of bitter war, they have never been settled by war. Although militant religions such as Islam and Christianity made many converts by the sword, they never succeeded in completely eliminating their rivals. Instead, religious wars eventually ended after terrible carnage, with the exhausted survivors still clinging to their respective systems of belief and concluding that they could, after all, co-exist. We are again learning the same painful lesson in Vietnam.

In the last analysis, ideological differences cannot be settled by force; the only way to stamp out an idea is to kill the last person who holds it, and even then it is apt to re-emerge. As a result, I believe that mutual tolerance for ideological differences will increase and that, insofar as they lead to conflicts, these will come to be fought primarily by psychological, political, and economic means, especially since each side realizes that attempts to resolve them by violence could easily lead to the extermination of both. The overriding task of our generation is to hasten the day when solutions to such conflicts will no longer be sought by resort to force, but by other means that hold out more hope of resolving them and assuring human survival.

SENATOR GEORGE S. MCGOVERN: Some difficult but persistent questions are being raised by a growing number of Americans: What can the individual citizen do about a national policy he believes to be wrong? Should a young man refuse to go to war? Should a taxpayer refuse to pay taxes? Should a Congressman vote against military appropriations?

The answer to these questions can be derived, at least in part, from our understanding, painful as it may be, that all Americans bear some measure of responsiblity for Vietnam. Considering the consequences of a decision or series of decisions to go to war, both to our own society and to the people who live in the battle area, no individual can justify apathy or inaction on the ground that the issues are so complex that he cannot form a valid judgment. There is a qualitative difference between issues of this magnitude and such matters as, for example, whether or not there should be a price support program for soybeans, where a certain amount of public indifference is understandable. And in any case, there is really no need to know the names of the villages, the significance of individual battles, the history of the region, or the identity of national leaders in order to reach a determination that the basic premises of our involvement in Vietnam are not valid.

Public officials should, therefore, be made to answer such legitimate questions as whether we have a real interest in the outcome of a conflict and, more importantly, whether we have a *right* to interfere. A refusal to answer on the basis of such considerations as "You'd support me if you knew what I know" is an abuse of power that a democratic society can never tolerate.

Regarding the form individual responsibility should take, I think it is possible to offer but one practical standard: to employ the means of expression that coincide with each individual's sense of propriety and good judgment. I cannot recommend to anyone that he violate the law, and none of us should recommend that a law, if it meets constitutional tests and has been properly enacted, should not be enforced, even if it is unwise. Yet I also find it impossible to sharply condemn anyone whose conscience impels him to take such steps as resisting the draft or refusing to pay war taxes and who is ready and willing to accept the personal and legal consequences of that action. If the Congress will not employ the orderly, legal means at its disposal for reversing a disastrous policy—and in that sense this war belongs to the Congress as much as to President Johnson or President Nixon—then perhaps we can understand, or perhaps even admire, those who believe essentially what many of us do, but who are willing to risk so much more in furtherance of the responsibility we all share.

I think we should hold in especially high esteem the young people who have been in the vanguard of protest against our Vietnam involvement. Some may find it necessary to distinguish between their physical tactics and their philosophical commitment. Most Americans probably cannot see themselves picketing, engaging in public demonstrations, or even raising their voices, so they cannot identify with protests that assume those forms. Yet they should recognize that vigorous objection to policies which the individual regards as unwise is the very stuff of which democracy is made. The true patriot follows the whole of Carl Schurz's admonition: "My country right or wrong; if right to be kept right, if wrong to be put right."

But if we all share the burden, if we all have some blood, both Vietnamese and American, on our hands, some of us must answer to a higher standard because our responsibility is more direct. For Members of Congress, for public officials, for the press—for these groups in particular, I believe there is a higher obligation than merely to seek the comfort and present the views of constituents, of bureaucratic superiors, or of an editor. It is axiomatic that the prudence of public opinion turns on the public's access to truth and the honesty of its leaders.

In these terms it is difficult, in a way, to welcome to the ranks of outspoken opposition to the Vietnam war those high-ranking figures who may have criticized it privately, but who have nonetheless maintained a public posture of support. In my view the sincere convert, who has reversed an earlier judgment in support of what he now says has been a mistaken course, is much more deserving of admiration. The secret critic, if he is a Presidential adviser or an official with high-level duties in foreign policy or defense, may think he can accomplish more by remaining at his post, hoping to change the nation's direction from the inside. But at some point it must become clear to him that the damage he does by helping to maintain a façade of unity and well-being heavily outweighs any influence he might have. When that point arrives, I think his loyalty to the President must rank far below his duty to the public trust, and he should share his judgments openly with the public.

Members of Congress—and especially of the Senate, to which the Constitution delegates specific authority over foreign policy—should meet a similar standard, and it should inspire not only their statements but their actions as well. In retrospect, I am not proud of having forcefully criticized the war in Vietnam for many years while at the same time voting for the appropriations that allowed it to be fought. There is a strong emotional argument for supporting our soldiers on the line with everything they need. But they are best supported by actions designed to bring them home and to limit the power of the Executive to demand their sacrifice in an ignoble venture. I have stopped voting for Vietnam war appropriations, and I shall not do so again.

I am not impressed with those of my colleagues who refused to join at all in the dissent over our Vietnam policy until the war went "sour" with the American public. It is the function of genuine leadership to lead, even at some political risk—not simply to react to the changing public mood. Senators and Representatives who remained silent about Vietnam in the 1960s must carry a troubled spirit about that silence today.

We should also recognize that the posture of the press is of paramount importance. I am convinced that some of the best American journalists can today claim credit for the mandate for change to which President Johnson responded in March, 1968—not because they argued for it but because they reported the facts. That turning point might have come much sooner had theirs not been rather lonely voices in the early months and years of our escalation.

The desire to be favored by news sources invites insidious pressures upon the journalist who knows that his access to officials and to information may be restricted if his reporting sheds critical light on national policies. Perhaps journalism needs more independence. In any event, each member of the profession should be guided by the principle recognized in the Constitutional safeguards of freedom of the press—the fact that an informed public is essential if democracy is to function. The Vice President should be roundly condemned for his attempts to intimidate the critical press. It should also be said that any newsman who is intimidated and who seeks new favor by omission of critical facts deserves equal condemnation. We can least afford to suspend the premises of the First Amendment where issues of war and peace are involved.

Our best efforts, then, should be aimed toward permanent incorporation of these attitudes into national awareness. If the Vietnam war has this result and if it brings about the philosophical and moral adjustments in our international affairs necessary to avoid future Vietnams, then we will have accomplished all that we can to justify the enormous toll it has taken in American flesh, treasure, and spirit.

MARCUS RASKIN: The American war in Southeast Asia raises the issue of civil disobedience for more Americans with each moment that it continues. Still, it is a little late to talk about sanctioning civil disobedience when the jails contain many draft resisters, when the war has driven many young people to flee the United States as political refugees, when soldiers desert in large numbers, and when some citizens attempt, in a somewhat pitiable way, to show their anger against the war by withholding taxes —and wind up paying interest to the Government for their efforts. It is not for us to make these activities legitimate or illegitimate. The dialectic between the individual and the state is a continuous one in history.

The real question is: Does the state itself live under law or does the state use the law? That, it seems to me, is the primary question that must be asked before we examine the problem of whether or not an eighteen-year-old should be prepared to destroy his conscience in order to be "civilly obedient."

Is law an instrument that those who wield the power of the state may use to conceal their conduct or exploit the weak? Are there no sanctions on a state which so transforms itself that it becomes an illegitimate organization, perpetrating mass murder and the destruction of one's own, or another's, culture? What can the citizen do? The Government is still able to commandeer taxes, control technology, recruit manpower, and at the same time "grant" conscientious objection to the few, "exempt" the middle class from service in imperial wars, and "permit" civil disobedience.

When the choice lies between a White House adviser who conceives, implements, or creates the circumstances for a series of My Lai incidents and the individual soldier or citizen who says no to such actions, it is the individual with whom we must stand. The burden of "expropriation" is always on the state, not on the individual or the community. As Hans Morgenthau has said, it is the soldier who says no to this war who serves the humanist values of America. The basic question in this war is one of statecraft. It is *not* one of conscience. It is whether the state itself intends to live under law.

The civics courses in our schools taught us that the state lived under the law and that those who held the power of the state—the rulers—were chosen by an active, participating people (not an immobile, passive mass) which would have the authority to impose restraints on those who wielded the power of the rulers. In this context we believed in the social contract: People got together and chose leadership and eventually changed it or rechose it. Those who did not believe this mythical—but overpowering—version of the social contract adopted an alternative version: They gave leadership power over their lives, that is, obeisance in exchange for protection.

Over this last generation both definitions of the social contract have been destroyed. Because of the concentration of power in the state hierarchy, with its control over military technology, the modern state can no longer give protection. In effect, it risks everyone's life constantly. The Cuban missile crisis is a profound example of that: A few people risked the lives of 500 million people without a bat of an eyelash. Once the few can risk the lives of the many at any moment simply because of forces in being and because there is no check among the people, the idea that people will remain pliant and obeisant is unrealistic. Because the state can no longer give protection, the question of whether or not obeisance should follow is very much in doubt in the minds of individual citizens.

The situation in which the entire legitimacy of the state is open to question results from its own illegal and life-threatening activities. We might think of two separate activities of the state that undermine its own legitimacy: the power to destroy everything and the willingness to exercise such power. In the Roman Empire, the emperor was followed around by a man whose task was to inform him that he was merely mortal, despite the cheers of the crowds. In the United States, on the other hand, the President is followed around by a man whose task, in effect, is to tell him he is immortal because he has the codes to unleash thermonuclear destruction on the world. This situation—the power to inflict mass destruction—*denies* the legitimacy of the state because it can act outside the law, on whim. This contradicts the idea of the social contract.

There is a second, more immediate sense in which the state's legitimacy is called into question, which is illuminated by the war in Southeast Asia. Historically, there was an idea of winning a war and then having peace. But a new idea for the United States—a central one for empire—developed after World War II: The matter of winning any particular war, or of losing it, became secondary to the quest for constant military engagement and the display of American power. War became a continuous way of life. War was no longer attached to interests, purposes, or objectives. It became an end in itself, prepared and conducted at the pleasure of national security institutions.

Since World War II, indeed, the primary activity of national security institutions has been to police the world. Law is subservient to the club, to napalm, to the bribe, to the rolling thunder of the B-52. The United States has executed scores of agreements, assigned hundreds of thousands of troops around the world, placed tactical and strategic nuclear weapons hither and yon, bought and sold governments. National security activity has become a criminal enterprise without political accountability or humane motive.

This situation begins to explain American policy, and simultaneously suggests its illegal nature and the disrepute in which it is held among the young. As we study the history of empires, we see that wars became their way of life. But with each successive generation the interest and commitment to war became less, because the purposes of the culture were increasingly questioned. This is happening today in American culture. Martial values do not impress young people in America as the meaning of our culture. A new generation of Americans has come to consciousness, convinced that authority cannot be based on threat, magic, and force. They say that the social contract —the organization of the body politic—must be predicated on persuasion and verification. In the absence of persuasion and verification, those who wield power have no claim to the exercise of legitimate authority.

How can the legitimacy of the social contract be restored? A first step would be for Congress to rid the Government of the curse of "classified information." Over the years a system of secrecy has been developed to keep from public view certain egregious activities of the national security apparatus while enforcing a standard of loyalty to *disloyal* acts on the part of the Government civil servant. What is required of Congress is to pull back the national security veil so that legal and moral judgments can be made about the nature of American policies and of threats, real or fanciful, which may be perceived within the Government. It seems to be an adage of power within the bureaucracy that the greater the power, the lower the legal and moral standards applied and the higher the secrecy classification.

I have already alluded to the arrangements and Executive agreements that have been made with and *in* other nations, which result in continuous engagement around the world. It is important to review those arrangements, as the Senate Committee on Foreign Relations has begun to do. But there is more to be done. Arrangements on paper reflect structural involvements in other countries. As the Administration pursues its doctrine of "low profile" involvement around the world, using the C.I.A. or foreign troops rather than American soldiers for intervention, the need for close and continuing public scrutiny becomes more urgent. There is a need, for example, for development of a new standard of bureaucratic responsiblity. Would it change the decisional process and the casual view of war if Government officials were personally responsible in a *legal* sense for their policy actions? Would we not gain much if the decisions made by Government were printed publicly in majority and minority opinions, much in the manner of a court decision, so that the people could begin to judge these decisions and act accordingly? If such questions are to be answered in a positive manner, the Congress and the people must redefine legitimacy, authority, and control over the governing apparatus. To put it another way, rather than the internal and national security institutions spying on the people, it is now time for the process to be reversed.

Congressman Reuss has suggested some ways of beginning to define the parameters of bureaucratic responsibility and individual action within a hierarchic structure. Some argue that one cannot expect to instill either personal or corporate responsiblity in people whose missions are defined through the bureaucratic chain of command. But the Nuremberg precedent holds otherwise, and so do resolutions of the United Nations assembly and provisions of the United States Military Code.

Should such activity proceed from the work of another commission? Public commissions give the troubled the feeling that something is being done. They are composed of prestigious names—liberal (not too liberal) members of the Establishment, bankers, foundation executives, Nobel laureates. If they were, at one time or another, members of a criminal enterprise involved in the cause of imperial domination, so much the better. Such commissions have lost their credibility. We must stop looking for that golden lining, the person or group who will save us. We must look to ourselves and to our own resources. Congress, for example, should develop a continuous commission to study the Vietnam war in and of itself and as a program that illumines the model of action the national security state will use in one form or another against other nations—and finally against Americans.

The techniques and programs developed for the edge of the empire end up as the course of treatment for our own citizenry. I would propose a group of commissions— of Congress and scholars, of people at their work places and at town meetings—to define the personal and corporate responsibility which we demand of our Government. Such commissions would begin to make clear that Secretaries of State, generals, and other high officials will have their missions critically examined, so that rules for action may be prescribed. Those institutions that are found to be capable only of criminal activity should be disbanded.

Finally, ways must be found to revive the moribund institutions of international law. One wonders why Congress could not pass a resolution asking a group of foreign nations to test the legality of the Vietnam war under the Nuremberg rules and the United Nations Charter.

There is a collision course in American society. Can it act on the basis of law, verification, and persuasion, or can it only rely on force and threat? Those who believe that authority can be based on law, persuasion, and verification must act now to put their convictions to the test. Or is it already too late? We shall see.

CHARLES C. MOSKOS, JR.: I would like to examine the question of responsibility for what happened at My Lai by looking at: (1) the attitudes and behavior of the combat GIs in Vietnam, and (2) the reaction of elite groups in our society as symbolized by many of the comments made by participants in this discussion. Both of these factors have ominous implications for the future of America's civil-military relations.

During the summers of 1965 and 1968, I took part—as a press correspondent—in numerous military operations and patrols in Vietnam. During these periods I witnessed the deaths and maimings of both Americans and Vietnamese. Cruel acts occurred on both sides with nauseating frequency. As a day-to-day participant in the combat situation, I was repeatedly struck by the brutal reactions of soldiers to their participation in the war. To understand the way in which combat soldiers' attitudes and behavior are shaped, however, one must try to comprehend the conditions under which they must manage. The misery of these conditions is so extreme that conventional moral standards are eclipsed in a way difficult for the noncombatant to appreciate. Much like the Hobbesian description of primitive life, the combat situation also reaches the state of being nasty, brutish, and short. Minute-by-minute survival is uppermost in the combat soldier's every thought and action. The ultimate standard rests on keeping alive—a harsh standard which can sanction atrocities.

First of all, there are the routine physical stresses of combat existence: the weight of the pack and armament, tasteless food, diarrhea, lack of water, leeches, mosquitoes, rain, torrid heat, mud, and loss of sleep. On top of this, the soldier not only faces the imminent danger of loss of life or limb, but also witnesses combat wounds and deaths suffered by his comrades. In an actual firefight with the enemy, the scene is generally one of utmost chaos and confusion. Deadening fear intermingles with acts of bravery and bestiality and, strangely enough, even moments of exhilaration. Moreover, even when not in battle, the presence of booby traps is a constant threat (according to Army statistics 65 per cent of casualties suffered in Vietnam are from such devices). Thus, the soldier's initial reluctance to endanger civilians is overcome by his fear

discussion may inadvertently add a few strokes. It would not be too far afield to say that antimilitarism has become the anti-Semitism of the intellectual community.

This state of affairs is reprehensible because it is a cheap way to misdirect attention away from the bases of America's adventuristic policies by melodramatically dealing with the byproducts of those policies. The blanket hostility toward military persons so endemic among most of my colleagues and students actually obscures the root causes of our country's malevolent actions. What must always be remembered is that the grievous chain of events that led us into Vietnam arose out of a broader Cold War and counterrevolutionary mentality that has been most forcefully articulated by civilian advisers and policy makers of putative liberal persuasion. The war in Vietnam is just one of many interventions of the United States against social revolutions throughout the Third World. Rather than shortsightedly castigating the men in uniform, it is the civilian militarists and the social system which produces them that ought to be the object of our critical concern.

It is with a deep sense of despair that I observe the justified opposition to the war in Vietnam being focused into a concerted attack on the armed forces *per se*. At the least, the concerned human being must always keep in mind the profound distinction between actions of individuals arising out of placement in particular situations —such as the My Lai's of war—and the structural and historical determinants which result in the creation of such situations. If our society is ever to fulfill its democratic promise, the relationship between its civilian and military structures requires especially sustained and intellectually honest attention. This will not be accomplished by scapegoating the military—whether for reasons of moral outrage or purposes of tactical expediency. Indeed, in many ways our American society has a much better military than it deserves.

The surge of antimilitarism at elite cultural and intellectual levels is occurring at a time when the whole framework of America's civil-military relations is undergoing fundamental change. More than a quarter-century ago, the noted political scientist Harold Lasswell first stated his theory of the garrison state. Forecasting a particular form of social organization, the garrison state would be characterized by the militarization of the civil order. The subordination of societal goals to the preparations for war would lead to the obliteration of the distinction between civilians and military personnel. The convergence of the armed forces and American society which began in World War II and continued through the Cold War decades of the 1950s and 1960s seemed, in certain respects, to confirm the emergence of the garrison state.

But the prospects for the 1970s require a reformulation of the garrison-state concept. For we are entering a time in which the armed forces are becoming more distinct and segmented from civilian society. A series of developments points to a growing isolation of the military from the mainstream of American life: the move toward an all-volunteer force at enlisted levels, the recruitment of officers from narrowing circles of the social spectrum, the de-emphasis of the Reserve and National Guard, the use of the military as an overt welfare agency for America's underclasses, and growing institutional autonomy within the military services. All this is happening at the same time that antimilitarism has become the new rage in the intellectual fashion world.

The divergence of armed forces and society will be reflected in closer and more critical scrutiny of the military's budgetary and force demands. But it is highly improbable that this new skepticism will result in any basic curtailment of the dominant role military procurement has come to play in our nation's economy, or that the United States will fundamentally alter what it considers to be its global interests. In fact, the institution of an all-volunteer, fully professional military force may mean that overseas interventionist policies will engender fewer political repercussions at home. Witness to this proposition is the acceleration of opposition to the war in Vietnam as the personal interests of articulate and vocal middle-class youth became involved.

The immediate future, then, points to a new phase in American civil-military relations. The character of the post-Vietnam period will be the conjunction of a still massive military force which will be socially unrepresentative and considered a pariah at elite cultural and intellectual levels. To rephrase Lasswell, it might be more accurate to speak of our society moving toward a *split-level garrison state*. This is to say that the imminent danger to a democratic society is not the specter of overt military control of national policy, but the more subtle one of a military isolated from the general citizenry, allowing for greater international irresponsibility by its civilian leaders. It is only when the consequences of such irresponsibility are uniformly felt throughout the body politic that we can begin to hope constraints will develop on the use of violence to implement national policy.

APPENDIXES

1. PRINCIPLES OF NUREMBERG

In 1945, at the initiative of the United States, the General Assembly of the United Nations affirmed unanimously "the principles of international law recognized by the Charter of the Nuremberg Tribunal." In 1950, the International Law Commission formulated the Principles of Nuremberg, which offer the most complete set of guidelines presently available on the relationship between personal responsibility and war crimes.

PRINCIPLE I
Any person who commits an act which constitutes a crime under international law is responsible therefor and liable to punishment.

PRINCIPLE II
The fact that internal law does not impose a penalty for an act which constitutes a crime under international law does not relieve the person who committed the act from responsibility under international law.

PRINCIPLE III
The fact that a person who committed an act which constitutes a crime under international law acted as Head of State or responsible Government official does not relieve him from responsibility under international law.

PRINCIPLE IV
The fact that a person acted pursuant to order of his Government or of a superior does not relieve him from responsibility under international law, provided a moral choice was in fact possible for him.

PRINCIPLE V
Any person charged with a crime under international law has the right to a fair trial on the facts and law.

PRINCIPLE VI
The crimes hereinafter set out are punishable as crimes under international law:

a. Crimes against peace:

(i) Planning, preparation, initiation or waging of a war of aggression or a war in violation of international treaties, agreements or assurances; '

(ii) Participation in a common plan or conspiracy for the accomplishment of any of the acts mentioned under (i).

b. War crimes:

Violations of the laws or customs of war which include, but are not limited to, murder, ill-treatment or deportation to slave-labour or for any other purpose of civilian population of or in occupied territory, murder or ill-treatment of prisoners of war or persons on the seas, killing of hostages, plunder of public or private property, wanton destruction of cities, towns, or villages, or devastation not justified by military necessity.

c. Crimes against humanity:

Murder, extermination, enslavement, deportation and other inhuman acts done against any civilian population, or persecutions on political, racial or religious grounds, when such acts are done or such persecutions are carried on in execution of or in connexion with any crime against peace or any war crime.

PRINCIPLE VII
Complicity in the commission of a crime against humanity as set forth in Principle VI is a crime under international law.

2. EXCERPTS FROM DEPARTMENT OF THE ARMY FIELD MANUAL, THE LAW OF LAND WARFARE

The following extracts are from Department of the Army Field Manual, No. 27-10, *The Law of Land Warfare*, published in 1956 by the U.S. Government Printing Office and distributed by the Office of the Judge Advocate General of the Department of the Army. The entire manual is based on the acceptance by the United States of the obligation to conduct warfare in accordance with the international law of war. The manual lists the twelve Hague and Geneva Conventions which have been properly ratified by the United States and are part of the supreme law of the land by virtue of Article VI of the United States Constitution.

1. *Purpose and Scope*

The purpose of this Manual is to provide authoritative guidance to military personnel on the customary and treaty law applicable to the conduct of warfare on land and to relationships between belligerents and neutral States. Although certain of the legal principles set forth herein have application to warfare at sea and in the air as well as to hostilities on land, this Manual otherwise concerns itself with the rules peculiar to naval and aerial warfare only to the extent that such rules have some direct bearing on the activities of land forces.

This Manual is an official publication of the United States Army. However, those provisions of the Manual which are neither statutes nor the text of treaties to which the United States is a party should not be considered binding upon courts and tribunals applying the law of war. However, such provisions are of evidentiary value insofar as they bear upon questions of customs and practice.

2. *Purposes of the Law of War*

The conduct of armed hostilities on land is regulated by the law of land warfare which is both written and unwritten. It is inspired by the desire to diminish the evils of war by:

a. Protecting both combatants and noncombatants from unnecessary suffering;

b. Safeguarding certain fundamental human rights of persons who fall into the hands of the enemy, particularly prisoners of war, the wounded and sick, and civilians; and

c. Facilitating the restoration of peace.

3. *Basic Principles*

a. Prohibitory Effect. The law of war places limits on the exercise of a belligerent's power in the interests mentioned in paragraph 2 and requires that belligerents refrain from employing any kind or degree of violence which is not actually necessary for military purposes and that they conduct hostilities with regard for the principles of humanity and chivalry.

The prohibitory effect of the law of war is not minimized by "military necessity," which has been defined as that principle which justifies those measures not forbidden by international law which are indispensable for securing the complete submission of the enemy as soon as possible. Military necessity has been generally rejected as a defense for acts forbidden by the customary and conventional laws of war inasmuch as the latter have been developed and framed with consideration for the concept of military necessity.

b. Binding on States and Individuals. The law of war is binding not only upon States as such but also upon individuals and, in particular, the members of their armed forces.

4. *Sources*

The law of war is derived from two principal sources:

a. Lawmaking Treaties (or Conventions), such as the Hague and Geneva Conventions.

b. Custom. Although some of the law of war has not been incorporated in any treaty or convention to which the United States is a party, this body of unwritten or customary law is firmly established by the custom of nations and well defined by recognized authorities on international law.

Lawmaking treaties may be compared with legislative enactments in the national law of the United States and the customary law of war with the unwritten Anglo-American common law. . . .

7. *Force of the Law of War*

a. Technical Force of Treaties and Position of the United States. Technically, each of the lawmaking treaties regarding the conduct of warfare is, to the extent established by its terms, binding only between the States that have ratified or acceded to, and have not thereafter denounced (withdrawn from), the treaty or convention and is binding only to the extent permitted by the reservations, if any, that have accompanied such ratification or accession on either side. The treaty provisions quoted in this manual in bold-face type are contained in treaties which have been ratified without reservation, except as otherwise noted, by the United States.

These treaty provisions are in large part but formal and specific applications of general principles of the unwritten law. While solemnly obligatory only as between the parties thereto, they may be said also to represent modern international public opinion as to how belligerents and neutrals should conduct themselves in the particulars indicated.

For these reasons, the treaty provisions quoted herein will be strictly observed and enforced by United States forces without regard to whether they are legally binding upon this country. Military commanders will be instructed which, if any, of the written rules herein quoted are not legally binding as between the United States and each of the States immediately concerned, and which, if any, for that reason are not for the time being to be observed or enforced.

b. Force of Treaties Under the Constitution. Under the Constitution of the United States, treaties constitute part of the "supreme Law of the Land" (art. VI, clause 2). In consequence, treaties relating to the law of war have a force equal to that of laws enacted by the Congress. Their provisions must be observed by both military and civilian personnel with the same strict regard for both the letter and spirit of the law which is required with respect to the Constitution and statutes enacted in pursuance thereof.

c. Force of Customary Law. The unwritten or customary

law of war is binding upon all nations. It will be strictly observed by United States forces, subject only to such exceptions as shall have been directed by competent authority by way of legitimate reprisals for illegal conduct of the enemy. The customary law of war is part of the law of the United States and, insofar as it is not inconsistent with any treaty to which this country is a party or with a controlling executive or legislative act, is binding upon the United States, citizens of the United States, and other persons serving this country.

8. *Situations to Which Law of War Applicable*

a. Types of Hostilities. War may be defined as a legal condition of armed hostility between States. While it is usually accompanied by the commission of acts of violence, a state of war may exist prior to or subsequent to the use of force. The outbreak of war is usually accompanied by a declaration of war.

Instances of armed conflict without declaration of war may include, but are not necessarily limited to, the exercise of armed force pursuant to a recommendation, decision, or call by the United Nations, in the exercise of the inherent right of individual or collective self-defense against armed attack, or in the performance of enforcement measures through a regional arrangement, or otherwise, in conformity with appropriate provions of the United Nations Charter.

b. Customary Law. The customary law of war applies to all cases of declared war or any other armed conflict which may arise between the United States and other nations, even if the state of war is not recognized by one of them. The customary law is also applicable to all cases of occupation of foreign territory by the exercise of armed force, even if the occupation meets with no armed resistance.

c. Treaties. Treaties governing land warfare are applicable to various forms of war and armed conflict as provided by their terms. The Hague Conventions apply to "war." Common Article 2 of the Geneva Conventions of 1949 states:

In addition to the provisions which shall be implemented in peacetime, the present Convention shall apply to all cases of declared war or of any other armed conflict which may arise between two or more of the High Contracting Parties, even if the state of war is not recognized by one of them.

The Convention shall also apply to all cases of partial or total occupation of the territory of a High Contracting Party, even if the said occupation meets with no armed resistance.

Although one of the Powers in conflict may not be a party to the present Convention, the Powers who are parties thereto shall remain bound by it in their mutual relations. They shall furthermore be bound by the Convention in relation to the said Power, if the latter accepts and applies the provisions thereof. . . .

9. *Applicability of Law of Land Warfare in Absence of a Declaration of War*

As the customary law of war applies to cases of international armed conflict and to the forcible occupation of enemy territory generally as well as to declared war in its strict sense, a declaration of war is not an essential condition of the application of this body of law. Similarly, treaties relating to "war" may become operative notwithstanding the absence of a formal declaration of war. . . .

11. *Civil War*

a. Customary Law. The customary law of war becomes applicable to civil war upon the recognition of the rebels as belligerents.

b. Geneva Conventions of 1949.

In the case of armed conflict not of an international character occurring in the territory of one of the High Contracting Parties, each Party to the conflict shall be bound to apply, as a minimum, the following provisions:

(1) Persons taking no active part in the hostilities, including members of armed forces who have laid down their arms and those placed hors de combat by sickness, wounds, detention or any other cause, shall in all circumstances be treated humanely, without any adverse distinction founded on race, colour, religion or faith, sex, birth or wealth, or any other similar criteria.

To this end, the following acts are and shall remain prohibited at any time and in any place whatsoever with respect to the abovementioned persons:

(a) violence to life and person, in particular murder of all kinds, mutilation, cruel treatment and torture;

(b) taking of hostages;

(c) outrages upon personal dignity, in particular, humiliating and degrading treatment;

(d) the passing of sentences and the carrying out of executions without previous judgment pronounced by a regularly constituted court, affording all the judicial guarantees which are recognized as indispensable by civilized peoples.

(2) The wounded and sick shall be collected and cared for. An impartial humanitarian body, such as the International Committee of the Red Cross, may offer its services to the Parties to the conflict.

The Parties to the conflict would further endeavor to bring into force, by means of special agreements, all or part of the other provisions of the present Convention. . . .

498. *Crimes Under International Law*

Any person, whether a member of the armed forces or a civilian, who commits an act which constitutes a crime under international law is responsible therefor and liable to punishment. Such offenses in connection with war comprise:

a. Crimes against peace.

b. Crimes against humanity.

c. War crimes.

Although this manual recognizes the criminal responsibility of individuals for those offenses which may comprise any of the foregoing types of crimes, members of the armed forces will normally be concerned only with those offenses constituting "war crimes."

499. *War Crimes*

The term "war crime" is the technical expression for a violation of the law of war by any person or persons, military or civilian. Every violation of the law of war is a war crime.

500. *Conspiracy, Incitement, Attempts, and Complicity*

Conspiracy, direct incitement, and attempts to commit, as well as complicity in the commission of, crimes against peace, crimes against humanity, and war crimes are punishable.

190 WAR CRIMES AND THE AMERICAN CONSCIENCE

501. *Responsibility for Acts of Subordinates*

In some cases, military commanders may be responsible for war crimes committed by subordinate members of the armed forces, or other persons subject to their control. Thus, for instance, when troops commit massacres and atrocities against the civilian population of occupied territory or against prisoners of war, the responsibility may rest not only with the actual perpetrators but also with the commander. Such a responsibility arises directly when the acts in question have been committed in pursuance of an order of the commander concerned. The commander is also responsible if he has actual knowledge, or should have knowledge, through reports received by him or through other means, that troops or other persons subject to his control are about to commit or have committed a war crime and he fails to take the necessary and reasonable steps to insure compliance with the law of war or to punish violators thereof. . . .

506. *Suppression of War Crimes*

a. Geneva Conventions of 1949. The Geneva Conventions of 1949 contain the following common undertakings:

The High Contracting Parties undertake to enact any legislation necessary to provide effective penal sanctions for persons committing, or ordering to be committed, any of the grave breaches of the present Convention defined in the following Article.

Each High Contracting Party shall be under the obligation to search for persons alleged to have committed or ordering to be committed, such grave breaches, and shall bring such persons, regardless of their nationality, before its own courts. It may also, if it prefers, and in accordance with the provisions of its own legislation, hand such persons over for trial to another High Contracting Party concerned, provided such High Contracting Party has made out a prima facie case.

Each High Contracting Party shall take measures necessary for the suppression of all acts contrary to the provisions of the present Convention other than the grave breaches defined in the following Article.

In all circumstances, the accused persons shall benefit by safe-guards of proper trial and defense, which shall not be less favoura-ble than those provided by Article 105 and those following of the Geneva Convention relative to the treatment of Prisoners of War of August 12, 1949.

b. Declaratory Character of Above Principles. The princi-ples quoted in *a*, above, are declaratory of the obligations of belligerents under customary international law to take measures for the punishment of war crimes committed by all persons, including members of a belligerent's own armed forces.

c. Grave Breaches. "Grave breaches" of the Geneva Con-ventions of 1949 and other war crimes which are committed by enemy personnel or persons associated with the enemy are tried and punished by United States tribunals as violations of international law.

If committed by persons subject to United States military law, these "grave breaches" constitute acts punishable under the Uniform Code of Military Justice. Moreover, most of the acts designated as "grave breaches" are, if committed within the United States, violations of domestic law over which the civil courts can exercise jurisdiction.

507. *Universality of Jurisdiction*

a. Victims of War Crimes. The jurisdiction of United States military tribunals in connection with war crimes is not limited to offenses committed against nationals of the United States but extends also to all offenses of this nature committed against nationals of allies and of cobelligerents and stateless persons.

b. Persons Charged with War Crimes. The United States normally punishes war crimes as such only if they are commit-ted by enemy nationals or by persons serving the interests of the enemy State. Violations of the law of war committed by persons subject to the military law of the United States will usually constitute violations of the Uniform Code of Military Justice and, if so, will be prosecuted under that Code. Violations of the law of war committed within the United States by other persons will usually constitute violations of federal or state criminal law and preferably will be prosecuted under such law. . . . Com-manding officers of United States troops must insure that war crimes committed by members of their forces against enemy personnel are promptly and adequately punished.

508. *Penal Sanctions*

The punishment imposed for a violation of the law of war must be proportionate to the gravity of the offense. The death penalty may be imposed for grave breaches of the law. Corporal punishment is excluded. Punishments should be deterrent, and in imposing a sentence of imprisonment it is not necessary to take into consideration the end of the war, which does not of itself limit the imprisonment to be imposed.

509. *Defense of Superior Orders*

a. The fact that the law of war has been violated pursuant to an order of a superior authority, whether military or civil, does not deprive the act in question of its character of a war crime, nor does it constitute a defense in the trial of the accused individual, unless he did not know and could not reasonably have been expected to know that the act ordered was unlawful. In all cases where the order is held not to constitute a defense to an allegation of a war crime, the fact that the individual was acting pursuant to orders may be considered in mitigation of punishment.

b. In considering the question whether a superior order constitutes a valid defense, the court shall take into consideration the fact that obedience to lawful military orders is the duty of every member of the armed forces; that the latter cannot be expected, in conditions of war discipline, to weigh scrupulously the legal merits of the orders received; that certain rules of warfare may be controversial; or that an act otherwise amounting to a war crime may be done in obedience to orders conceived as a measure of reprisal. At the same time it must be borne in mind that members of the armed forces are bound to obey only lawful orders.

510. *Government Officials*

The fact that a person who committed an act which constitutes a war crime acted as the head of a State or as a responsible government official does not relieve him from responsibility for his act.

511. *Acts Not Punished in Domestic Law*
The fact that domestic law does not impose a penalty for an act which constitutes a crime under international law does not relieve the person who committed the act from responsibility under international law. . . .

3. TREATIES TO WHICH THE UNITED STATES IS A PARTY

The following international conventions relate to the conduct of war and have been signed and ratified by the United States:

1. Hague Convention No. III of 18 October 1907, Relative to the Opening of Hostilities.
2. Hague Convention No. IV of 18 October 1907, Respecting the Laws and Customs of War on Land, and the Annex thereto, embodying the Regulations Respecting the laws and Customs of War on Land.
3. Hague Convention No. V of 18 October 1907, Respecting the Rights and Duties of Neutral Powers and Persons in Case of War on Land.
4. Hague Convention No. IX of 18 October 1907, Concerning Bombardment by Naval Forces in Time of War.
5. Hague Convention No. X of 18 October 1907, for the Adaptation to Maritime Warfare of the Principles of the Geneva Convention.
6. Geneva Convention Relative to the Treatment of Prisoners of War of 27 July 1929.
7. Geneva Convention for the Amelioration of the Condition of the Wounded and Sick of Armies in the Field of 27 July 1929.
8. Treaty on the Protection of Artistic and Scientific Institu-

tions and Historic Monuments of 15 April 1935, cited as the *Roerich Pact.* Only the United States and a number of the American Republics are parties to this treaty.

9. Geneva Convention for the Amelioration of the Condition of the Wounded and Sick in Armed Forces in the Field of 12 August 1949.

10. Geneva Convention for the Amelioration of the Condition of Wounded, Sick and Shipwrecked Members of Armed Forces at Sea of 12 August 1949.

11. Geneva Convention Relative to the Treatment of Prisoners of War of 12 August 1949.

12. Geneva Convention Relative to the Protection of Civilian Persons in Time of War of 12 August 1949.

4. EXCERPTS FROM THE SUPREME COURT OPINION IN THE MATTER OF YAMASHITA

General Tomoyuki Yamashita was the commanding general of the Fourteenth Army Group of the Imperial Japanese Army in the Philippine Islands at the end of World War II. Following his surrender to American forces, a U.S. military commission tried him for violating the law of war by failing to control the operations of his troops, "permitting them to commit" atrocities against civilians and prisoners of war. There was no evidence that Yamashita had ordered the atrocities, or had even known about them. Nonetheless, he was convicted and sentenced to death. The Supreme Court of the United States affirmed the judgment on February 4, 1946, in a decision that included the following language:

The question then is whether the law of war imposes on an army commander a duty to take such appropriate measures as are within his power to control the troops under his command for the prevention of the specified acts which are violations of the law of war and which are likely to attend the occupation of hostile territory by an uncontrolled soldiery, and whether he may be charged with personal responsibility for his failure to take such measures when violations result. That this was the precise issue to be tried was made clear by the statements of the prosecution at the opening of the trial.

It is evident that the conduct of military operations by troops whose excesses are unrestrained by the orders or efforts of their commander would almost certainly result in violations which it is the purpose of the law of war to prevent. Its purpose to protect civilian populations and prisoners of war from brutality would largely be defeated if the commander of an invading army could with impunity neglect to take reasonable measures for their protection. Hence the law of war presupposes that its violation is to be avoided through the control of the operations of war by commanders who are to some extent responsible for their subordinates.

5. MAJORITY JUDGMENT OF THE TOKYO WAR CRIMES TRIBUNAL

The Majority Judgment of the Tokyo War Crimes Tribunal, handed down in November, 1948, affirmed the principle that political leaders who authorize illegal battlefield practices and policies, or who have knowledge of these practices and policies, are responsible for the commission of war crimes. The following is an excerpt from the Majority Judgment:

A member of a Cabinet which collectively, as one of the principal organs of the Government, is responsible for the care of prisoners is not absolved from responsibility if, having knowledge of the commission of the crimes in the sense already discussed, and omitting or failing to secure the taking of measures to prevent the commission of such crimes in the future, he elects to continue as a member of the Cabinet. This is the position even though the Department of which he has the charge is not directly concerned with the care of prisoners. A Cabinet member may resign. If he has knowledge of ill-treatment of prisoners, is powerless to prevent future ill-treatment of prisoners, but elects to remain in the Cabinet thereby continuing to participate in its collective responsibility for protection of prisoners he willingly assumes responsibility for any ill-treatment in the future.

Army or Navy commanders can, by order, secure proper treatment and prevent ill-treatment of prisoners. So can Ministers of War and of the Navy. If crimes are committed against prisoners under their control, of the likely occurrence of which they had, or should have had knowledge in advance, they are responsible for those crimes. If, for example, it be shown that within the units under his command conventional war crimes have been committed of which he knew or should have known, a commander who takes no adequate steps to prevent the occurrence of such crimes in the future will be responsible for such future crimes.

Notes on
the Contributors

HANNAH ARENDT is University Professor of political philosophy at the New School for Social Research in New York. She has taught at the University of California at Berkeley, Columbia University, and the University of Chicago, and was the first woman appointed to a full professorship at Princeton University. A contributor to numerous periodicals, she is the author of *The Origins of Totalitarianism, On Revolution, Between Past and Future, Eichmann in Jerusalem,* and the recently published *On Violence.*

JAMES ARMSTRONG is Bishop of the Dakotas area for the United Methodist Church. He was a member of the American study team sent to Vietnam in 1969 under interfaith sponsorship to study the problem of religious and political repression in Vietnam. The team included representatives of the major churches, as well as political and military experts, and issued a widely publicized report of its findings. He has contributed to many magazines and journals.

RICHARD J. BARNET is co-director of the Institute for Policy Studies in Washington, D. C. A graduate of the Harvard University Law School, he has served as a consultant to the Department of Defense and as a special assistant in the U.S. Arms Control and Disarmament Agency. He visited North Vietnam in November, 1969, as a member of the American Lawyers Committee to obtain perspective on the war from the other side. A frequent contributor to the *New York Review of Books* and other periodicals, he is the author of *Who Wants Disarmament?, Intervention and Revolution,* and *The Economy of Death.*

JONATHAN B. BINGHAM was elected to the United States House of Representatives in 1964. A Democrat-Liberal from New York City, he has served as secretary to Governor Averell Harriman of New York, as United States representative to the Economic and Social Council of the United Nations, and as the principal adviser to Ambassador Adlai Stevenson in economic and social affairs. He is the author of *Shirt Sleeve Diplomacy: Point 4 in Action.* He is a member of the Committee on Foreign Affairs and the Committee on House Administration.

GEORGE E. BROWN, JR., was elected to the United States House of Representatives in 1962. A Democrat from Los Angeles County, he was employed by the city of Los Angeles for twelve years in engineering and management. He is a member of the House Science and Astronautics Committee and of the Foreign Policy Steering Committee of the Democratic Study Group.

PHILLIP BURTON was elected to the United States House of Representatives in 1964. A Democrat from San Francisco, he was elected to the California State Assembly in 1956 as the youngest member and the only Democrat to defeat an incumbent Republican in California that year. He is a member of the House Committee on Education and Labor.

BENJAMIN V. COHEN practices law in Washington, D.C., and has held many posts in the Federal Government. While serving as general counsel to the Office of War Mobilization from 1943 to 1945, he was legal adviser to the International Monetary Conference at Breton Wood, N.H., and a member of the American delegation to the Dumbarton Oaks Conference. He was counsellor of the Department of State from 1945 to 1947, and was a member of the American delegation to the Berlin Conference (1945), a senior adviser to the American delegation to the United Nations General Assembly in London and New York (1946), and a member of the American delegation to the Paris Peace Conference (1946). A member of the U.S. delegation to the United Nations General Assembly (1947–1952), he was the

U.S. representative before the International Court of Justice in 1950, and a representative to the U.N. Disarmament Commission in 1952. He is the author of *The United Nations: Constitutional Development, Growth and Possibilities,* and *The United Nations in its Twentieth Year.*

JOHN CONYERS, JR., was elected to the United States House of Representatives in 1964. A Democrat from Detroit, Michigan, he had been a labor attorney and had worked with Dr. Martin Luther King, Jr., in the civil rights movement. He organized three fact-finding missions of Congressmen who went to Alabama in 1965 and Mississippi in 1966 and 1967 to investigate violations of civil and voting rights. A veteran of the Korean war, he was a member of the American study team that visited Vietnam in June, 1969, to investigate religious and political repression by the South Vietnamese government. He is a member of the House Committee on the Judiciary, and has written extensively on the role of blacks in American politics.

WILLIAM R. CORSON is a retired Marine lieutenant colonel who was head of the Marine Corps "Combined Action" pacification program in Vietnam in 1966 and 1967. His book on the Vietnam war, *The Betrayal,* was published in 1968 at the time of his retirement. Since then he has been a lecturer in economics at Howard University in Washington, D.C., and now is a vice-president of Operations Research, Inc., in Maryland. In addition to writing and lecturing on problems of insurgency and revolution, he has recently published a new book, *Promise or Peril,* which deals with the problems of black college students.

ROBERT C. ECKHARDT was elected to the United States House of Representatives in 1966. A Democrat from Harris County, Texas, he practiced law and was a member of the Texas House of Representatives. He is a member of the House Committee on Interstate and Foreign Commerce.

DON EDWARDS was elected to the United States House of Representatives in 1962. He is a Democrat from San Jose, California.

A former naval intelligence officer and F.B.I. agent, he is a past president of Americans for Democratic Action and has been active in civil liberties causes. He is a member of the Committee on Judiciary.

DANIEL ELLSBERG is a senior researcher associate at the Institute for International Studies at Massachusetts Institute of Technology. From 1967 until September, 1970, he was a Vietnam analyst for the RAND Corporation in Santa Monica, California. He is a graduate of Harvard University with a Ph.D. in economics. In 1964 and 1965 he was special assistant to the Assistant Secretary of Defense for International Security Affairs, working on Vietnam affairs. He joined the State Department in 1965 to go to Vietnam as a member of General Edward G. Lansdale's liaison office. From December, 1966, to June, 1967, he was special assistant to the Deputy U.S. Ambassador in Vietnam, with responsibility for evaluating pacification.

RICHARD A. FALK is professor of international law at Princeton University. He has been research director of the North American Section of the World Order Models Project, and was a faculty member at the Center for Advanced Study in the Behavioral Sciences at Stanford University, California. He acted as counsel before the International Court of Justice at the Hague in the Southwest Africa Cases. He is a member of the bar of the state of New York. His many works on international law and world order include *Law, War and Morality in the Contemporary World, The Role of Courts in the International Legal Order, Security Through Disarmament* (with Richard Barnet), *The Strategy of World Order, The Vietnam War and International Law, Legal Order in a Violent World,* and *The Status of Law in International Society.*

JEROME D. FRANK is professor of psychiatry at the Medical School of Johns Hopkins University. He is a past president of the Society for the Psychological Study of Social Issues, and since 1966 has been a member of the Social Science Advisory Board of the Arms Control and Disarmament Agency. The author of many articles on psychotherapy and other contributions to professional journals, he is the author of *Sanity and Survival: Psychological Aspects of War and Peace.*

DONALD M. FRASER was elected to the United States House of Representatives in 1962. He is a Democratic-Farmer-Laborite and was a state senator from 1954 to 1962. He is a member of the House Committee on Foreign Affairs and is chairman of the Democratic Study Group, the liberal caucus of House Democrats.

ARTHUR W. GALSTON is professor of biology at Yale University and director of the Marsh Botanical Gardens there. He is a past president of the Botanical Society of America and of the American Society of Plant Physiologists, and was a member of the Metabolic Biology Panel of the National Science Foundation. He is a consultant for the Central Research Department of E. I. du Pont de Nemours & Co., and is a member of the National Research Council. He is an expert in the study of the chemical control of plant growth and has testified before Congressional committees investigating the biological effects of the use of herbicides in Vietnam. He is the author of *Principles of Plant Physiology, The Life of the Green Plant,* and the forthcomig *Control Mechanisms in Plant Development.* He has published more than 100 scientific papers since 1943.

PRISCILLA HOLMES practices law in Washington, D. C. Formerly with the Washington law firms of Covington and Burling and Arnold and Porter, she is now working on an independent project dealing with legal aspects of war crimes.

ROBERT W. KASTENMEIER was elected to the United States House of Representatives in 1958. He is a Democrat from Madison, Wisconsin. Formerly a practicing attorney, he is a member of the House Judiciary Committee. In 1965 he conducted local hearings on American Vietnam policy and published *Hearings on Vietnam: Voices from the Grassroots.*

GABRIEL KOLKO is professor of history at the State University of New York at Buffalo. A graduate of Harvard University with a Ph.D. in history, he was an associate professor of history at the University of Pennsylvania. Professor Kolko's *Politics of War, 1943–45* was published in 1969 and widely reviewed as an important analysis of American foreign policy and the origins of the Cold War. He is also the author of the *Triumph of Conservatism 1900–1916, Railroads and Regulation, The Roots of American Foreign Policy,* and *Wealth and Power in America,* a study of the economic structure.

FRANK KOWALSKI, a retired colonel in the U.S. Army, served in Congress from 1958 to 1962 as a Representative from Connecticut. He is a graduate of the U.S. Military Academy at West Point and did graduate work at the Massachusetts Institute of Technology and Columbia University. During his Army career he was director of a program for disarmament of Germany, chief of staff of the U.S. Advisory group in Japan, and commandant of the U. S. Army Command Management School. While in Congress he served on the House Armed Services Committee. He was a member of the Subversive Activities Control Board from 1963 to 1967. He is the author of *Rearmament of Japan,* published in 1969.

ROBERT JAY LIFTON is professor of psychiatry at Yale University. He has served as a faculty member of the Washington School of Psychiatry, as a research associate in the Department of Psychiatry at Harvard University, and as an associate at the Harvard Center for East Asian studies. His work in the field of psychohistory—the relationship between individual psychology and historical change—is widely known, particularly his study of the survivors of Hiroshima, *Death in Life.* He is now the coordinator of a study group on the psychohistorical process. His other books include *Thought Reform and the Psychology of Totalism: a Study of Brainwashing in China, Revolutionary Immortality: Mao Tse-Tung and the Chinese Cultural Revolution,* and *History and Human Survival.* He edited *The Woman in America* and *America and the Asian Revolution.*

GORDON LIVINGSTON is a resident in psychiatry at Johns Hopkins Hospital in Baltimore, Maryland. A graduate of the U.S. Military Academy at West Point and the Johns Hopkins School of Medicine, he served in Vietnam as a major and was assigned as regimental surgeon to the Eleventh Armored Cavalry Regiment commanded by Colonel George Patton III. His "Letter from a Vietnam Veteran" and "The Blackhorse Prayer" were published in the *Saturday Review* in 1969.

MICHAEL MACCOBY is the director of the Project on Technology, Work and Character sponsored by the Harvard University Program on Technology and Society. He received his Ph.D. from Harvard University in social psychology and personality, and has taught at the University of Chicago, Harvard University's Department of Social Relations, and the Mexican Institute of Psychoanalysis. He has served on the faculty and board of directors of CIDOC in Cuernavaca, Mexico. Under the direction of Erich Fromm he conducted a socio-psychological study of a Mexican village from 1960 to 1967. He is a psychoanalyst in private practice and a visiting fellow at the Institute for Policy Studies. A contributor to periodicals and professional journals, he is the author (with Erich Fromm) of *Social Character in a Mexican Village.*

GEORGE S. MCGOVERN was elected to the United States Senate in 1962. A Democrat from South Dakota, he holds a Ph.D. in history and is a former professor of history and government at Dakota Wesleyan University, Mitchell, S. D. After serving in the United States House of Representatives from 1957 to 1961, he was named Food for Peace Director and Special Assistant to President Kennedy in 1961. He is chairman of the Senate Committee on Nutrition and Human Needs, and was a candidate for the Democratic presidential nomination in the summer of 1968.

STEWART MEACHAM is the director of the Peace Education Division of the American Friends Service Committee. He was in South Vietnam in 1967 to evaluate AFSC programs there, and in 1968 went to Hanoi to facilitate the release of three captured

United States pilots. He joined the American Friends Service Committee in 1957 after leaving the National Labor Relations Board. He has been active in the antiwar movement as both an organizer and an educator.

ABNER J. MIKVA was elected to the United States House of Representatives in 1968. A Democrat from Chicago, he has practiced law since 1952, was a member of the Illinois State Legislature for ten years, and was chairman of the Illinois House Judiciary Committee. He is a member of the House Committee on the Judiciary.

HANS MORGENTHAU is professor of political science and modern history at the University of Chicago and director of the Center for the Study of American Foreign and Military Policy. He has been a visiting professor at the University of California at Berkeley, Harvard University, Northwestern University, Columbia, Yale, and the Institute for Advanced Study at Princeton. A consultant to the Department of State and the Department of Defense, he is the author of many books on international politics. Among them are *Politics Among Nations, The Purpose of American Politics, In Defense of the National Interest, Politics in the Twentieth Century,* and *A New Foreign Policy for the United States.*

CHARLES C. MOSKOS, JR., is professor of sociology and chairman of the sociology department at Northwestern University in Evanston, Illinois. In 1969 and 1970 he did field research with the United Nations peacekeeping forces in Cyprus. He visited Vietnam in 1964 and 1967 as an observer in the combat zone, and published many articles on American combat soldiers in Vietnam. A frequent contributor to professional journals and popular magazines on topics of military sociology, he is the author of The *Sociology of Political Independence* and *The American Enlisted Man.*

PHILIP NOEL-BAKER is a Member of the British Parliament and

chairman of the Foreign Affairs Group of the Labor Party. Awarded the Nobel Peace Prize in 1959, he has served as a member of the League of Nations Secretariat, Parliamentary private secretary to the Secretary of State for Foreign Affairs (1929–1931), a member of the British delegation to the League of Nations, principal assistant to the President of the Disarmament Conference in Geneva (1932–1933), and Secretary of State for Commonwealth Relations (1947–1950). He has held university lecture positions and is the author of many books and articles on disarmament. Among his principal books are *The Geneva Protocol, Disarmament and the Coolidge Conference, The Private Manufacture of Armaments,* and *The Arms Race: A Programme for World Disarmament.*

EDWARD M. OPTON, JR., is senior research psychologist and associate dean of the Graduate School at the Wright Institute in Berkeley, California. He received his B.A. from Yale and his Ph.D. in 1964 from Duke University. While on leave from the University of California, Berkeley, he visited Vietnam in 1967 and 1968 as a reporter for the Pacifica Foundation radio stations.

LOUIS POLLAK is former dean of the Law School at Yale University. He joined the law faculty at Yale in 1953 after two years as legal counselor in the State Department. He is a director of the N.A.A.C.P. Legal Defense and Educational Fund and an expert in the fields of constitutional law and civil liberties. He was formerly editor-in-chief of the *Yale Law Journal* and is the editor of *The Constitution and the Supreme Court: A Documentary History.*

MARCUS RASKIN is co-director of the Institute for Policy Studies, Washington, D. C. He served as legislative counsel to twelve Democratic Congressmen from 1958 to 1961 and was staff editor of *The Liberal Papers,* published in 1961. A member of the National Security Council staff from 1961 to 1962, he served as education adviser in the Office of the President and was a member of the United States Disarmament Delegation in Geneva. He is the author of *Vietnam Reader* (with Bernard Fall) and of the forthcoming *Being and Doing*.

HENRY S. REUSS was elected to the United States House of Representatives in 1954. A Democrat from Milwaukee, he is a graduate of Cornell University and the Harvard Law School, and was deputy counsel to the Marshall Plan in Paris. He is the author of *The Critical Decade: An Economic Policy for America and the Free World* and *Revenue Sharing*. He serves on the Joint Economic Committee, the House Banking and Currency Committee, and the Committee on Government Operations, and is chairman of three House subcommittees.

BENJAMIN S. ROSENTHAL was elected to the United States House of Representatives in 1962. A Democrat from Queens, New York, he is a member of the Foreign Affairs Committee and Government Operations Committee. He is chairman of the Special Consumer Inquiry and is the principal sponsor of legislation to create a Department of Consumer Affairs.

WILLIAM FITTS RYAN was elected to the United States House of Representatives in 1960. He is a Democrat-Liberal from New York City and is one of the founders of the New York Democratic Reform Movement. An assistant district attorney for New York from 1950 to 1957, he was the Reform Democratic candidate for Mayor of New York City in 1965. He is a member of the Committee on the Judiciary and the Committee on Interior and Insular Affairs.

JONATHAN SCHELL is a writer for *The New Yorker* magazine. He is a graduate of Harvard University and has pursued graduate studies in Japan. He visited Vietnam in 1967 and traveled extensively throughout the country. His articles "The Village of Ben Suc" and "Quang Ngai and Quang Tin" are ranked among the finest reporting on the war. They have been published in book form under the titles *The Village of Ben Suc* and *The Military Half*.

JOHN B. SHEERIN, C.S.P., is a member of the order of Paulist Fathers and is editor-in-chief of *The Catholic World,* the oldest Catholic magazine in the United States. His column, *Sum and Substance,* is published in twenty-three Catholic newspapers. A graduate of Fordham Law School, he is a member of the bar of the state of New York. He served on the American Bishops' Press Panel at the Second Vatican Council and was moderator of the Panel at the Council's second session in 1963. He is a member of the steering committee of Clergy and Laymen Concerned About Vietnam, and was a co-author of *In the Name of America.*

PHILIP STERN was Deputy Assistant Secretary of State for Public Affairs in 1961 and 1962, and has been legislative assistant to Senators Paul Douglas and Henry Jackson. He served on the campaign staff of Adlai Stevenson in 1952, and was director of research for the Democratic National Committee and senior editor of the *Democratic Digest* from 1953 to 1956. A former editor and publisher of *The Northern Virginia Sun,* he is the author of *The Great Treasury Raid,* a well-known book on tax loopholes; *The Shame of a Nation,* a photographic essay on poverty; *Oh, Say Can You See: A Bifocal Tour of Washington,* a photographic exposition of the two faces of the Capital; and the recently published book, *The Oppenheimer Case: Security on Trial.*

TELFORD TAYLOR is professor of law at the Law School of Columbia University in New York. During World War II he was an Army intelligence officer in the European Theater, and from 1946 to 1949 he was a brigadier general and chief prosecutor for the United States at the Nuremberg War Crimes Tribunal. He holds the Distinguished Service Medal and decorations from the British, Dutch, French, and Polish governments. He is the author of many articles on political, legal, and military subjects and of the following books: *Sword and Swastika, Grand Inquest, The March of Conquest,* and *The Breaking Wave.*

WILLIAM P. THOMPSON is the chief executive officer (Stated

Clerk) of the General Assembly of the United Presbyterian Church in the United States of America. An attorney by profession, he is a member of the Kansas state bar. During World War II, he served as a lawyer in the office of the Staff Judge Advocate of the Air Transport Command, and was an assistant prosecutor in the trial of Prime Minister Tojo and other leading figures during the Tokyo War Crimes Trials.

GEORGE WALD is professor of biology at Harvard University. A recipient of the Nobel Prize in medicine in 1967, he specializes in biochemical evolution. He has taught at New York University, Columbia University, and the University of California, and has been a consultant to the Office of Naval Research and the Office of Scientific Research and Development. The recipient of many professional awards and medals, he has recently written extensively on ecological and environmental problems.